MEMORIAL SERVICES FOR WOMEN

Meg Bowman, PhD

D1546024

Sponsored by:
Women & Religion Task Force
A Committee of the
Pacific Central District
Unitarian Universalist Association

MEMORIAL SERVICES FOR WOMEN
©Meg Bowman
Third Printing
ISBN # 0-940483-01-7

Memorial Services for Women
is available from:
HOT FLASH PRESS
Box 21506
San Jose, CA 95151

Discount rate on all books:
  8 - 24 copies — 10%
25 - 36 copies — 20%
37 - 60 copies — 30%
over 60 copies — 40%

CA residents please add 7% sales tax.

Also distributed by Hot Flash Press:

Readings for Women's Programs (to open and close your meetings)
@$5.95 ea. plus $1 p/h

Dramatic Readings on Feminist Issues ©$10.95 ea. plus $1 p/h

Our Stunning Harvest: Dramatic Reading (adaptation of Ellen Bass' powerful peace poem) @$4.95 ea. plus $1 p/h.

DEATH

No more to see you
Oh, never more.
My heart breaks
My life is limp.
You, my love.
No more to see you
Oh, never more.

ACKNOWLEDGEMENTS:

As a Humanist Counselor, I perform weddings and other rites of passage. While planning a memorial service for a friend, I suddenly realized there was practically no material in print for feminists, non-believers and others whose beliefs do not fit into such neatly structured categories as "Christian," "Theist," or other orthodox classifications. Most funereal material is taken from traditional dogma and was written for men.

These readings may be used by and for women (and men) of a broad spectrum of beliefs; we all need poems, essays, responsive readings and songs to ease the grieving process. Feel free to reverse the gender in these readings and to make copies of any responsive reading you choose for a service; please give credit to the author. Responsive readings may, of course, be read as prose by a single reader.

The last pages of this book have a form for *you* to fill out so that your family will know *your* wishes. Let someone know when you have completed it and where it is kept.

Thanks to Marylou Hadditt, Arnold Crompton, Carl Seaburg, Daniel Panger, David Sammons, Mary Heath-Walter, Ted Ruhig, Bruce Southworth, Ward and Barbara Tabler, Alice Wallace, and others for their contributions. A special thanks to the Women and Religion Task Force, Pacific Central District — especially Alice Wallace, Rosemary Matson, Gail Hamaker, Charolotte Suskind, Mary Heath-Walter and Roderick Heath-Walter — who helped put it all together one lovely afternoon in beautiful Carmel Valley.

Meg Bowman
San Jose, CA
1984/1987

TABLE OF CONTENTS

A MOTHER'S GRAVE: Hattie Goff Burnett was the daughter of North Star, a Native American woman of the California Miwok tribe, who married an early California pioneer. Hattie, who was married to Thomas Hart Burnett, a nephew of California's first Governor, Peter H. Burnett, bore six children, then died of pneumonia at the age of 35. Unable to care for the children, Burnett sent them to boarding school at Sherman Institute, a Bureau of Indian Affairs school at Riverside, Calif. The oldest daughter, Winona, wrote a letter to her "Dear Dead Mama," and this was later inscribed on the grave marker. The grave is located on a hill at Goff Station, near Exchequer Dam in Merced County. *Photo by Joan B. Mayer*

A LEAVETAKING

Some have left
and others are about to leave;
so why should we be sorry
that we too must go?
And yet our hearts are sad
that on this mighty road
the friends we meet can set
no place to meet again.

                    —from the Sanskrit
                    (circa 1200 B.C.E.)

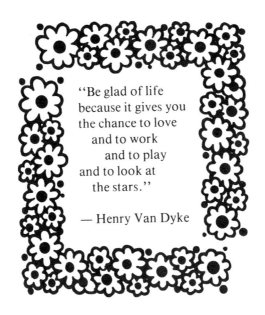

"Be glad of life
because it gives you
the chance to love
and to work
    and to play
and to look at
    the stars."

— Henry Van Dyke

A HUMANIST SERVICE: WHEN THE TIME COMES

*In the October issue of **The Atlantic** (1975), William Manchester, writing of the last years of H.L. Mencken, recalls his "lamenting the fact that there was no decent memorial service for non-believers." Such need no longer be the case. The humanist memorial service given for Lillie V. Tabler, pioneer woman suffragist member of the Fellowship of Humanity, Charter member of the Consumers Co-operative, and one of the founders of the first pensioners' union, was as follows:*

GOOD GRIEF

The Memorial which focuses on the eulogy warps reality; the one which summarizes statistics is as impersonal as words in an obituary notice. Music, and readings from relevant, beautiful prose and poetry can brighten the occasion. Description and anecdote can personalize the event. Humor can engrave it on the memory as a unique and wonderful experience of *Good* Grief.

My mother died on July 30, 1975, almost 98 years old, and her ashes were scattered over the Pacific, off the coast of Monterey. In the evening on August 6, a private service in her memory was held in my home. My brother, Paul, and 10 relatives and very close friends sat in a relaxed circle. We enjoyed a snack of tea, coffee, and pie.

Then, when we were ready, I said that my mother had enjoyed a long, active, productive life, that time had confined her to a chair on wheels, dulled her hearing, veiled her sight, and that she had said more than once, "I think it's time to go."

I told of how Mom and I had discussed death; of our agreement that the American Indian metaphor, "Returning to the loving arms of our Earth Mother," was an inviting image; of our pledge to welcome the lullabye, when the Owl called our names, knowing that life and love and death are one, even as the rain and river and sea are one. I recalled a few of my mother's humorous remarks, of her comments about creeping old age, and the necessity of submitting to the inevitable, and her smiling, "But I'll prevent it as long as I can." And she did.

Then suggesting that others recall something personal,

something touching, something humorous to share with the group, I sat back and waited. It was like a Quaker meeting. First one person, then another, related anecdotes; each person shared, some more than once. Every contribution evoked a chuckle, and, by association, another happy recollection. And where there were tears, they were not from grief at losing, but from joy at having known and loved this remarkable woman whose political leadership for welfare reform, minority rights, and women's liberation had inspired participatory support, whose uncomplaining endurance had commanded admiration, whose off-beat responses had evoked laughter.

This Memorial experiment illustrates the healing effect of humor. It is an example of *Good* Grief as distinguished from painful grief. *Good* Grief results from "letting go" and not losing; painful grief results from losing and "not letting go." Of course, every Memorial service must be unique, adapted to time, place, occasion, and to meeting the needs of the people present. But there is no doubt that creative interchange of appropriate personal anecdotes, in the service, can bring a smile to the heart, and that smile can be as healing as tears in dealing with grief.

— Ward Tabler

First printed in *Free Mind*, Sept.-Oct. 1975

The main goal in life is to live —
   to live fully and joyously . . .
   aware of all the possibilities
   life has to offer.

OUR LIVES CAN BE AN ACCIDENT
OR AN ADVENTURE.
THE CHOICE IS OURS.

Life is the opposite of death, and thoughts of death are necessary if we are to think significantly of life.

—Rollo May

BETWEEN US AND DEATH THERE IS ONLY LIFE,
WHICH IS THE FRAILEST THING IN THE WORLD.

MY MOTHER

One came and said to the Prophet: My mother has died, what shall I do for the good of her soul?

The Prophet thought of the panting heat of the desert, and he replied: Dig a well, that the thirsty may have water to drink.

The man dug the well and said: This have I done for my mother.

— Islamic

A MEMORIAL SERVICE

When planning a memorial service, plan it for the living — for family and friends. As you reflect on the values and life of the deceased, select songs, poems and responsive readings which are appropriate, and decide on the order of the presentations. Those who sing or read may need to rehearse. To make the service more meaningful, try to arrange a service which is original and is a reflection of the person being commemorated; make it a celebration of her life. If the deceased has let her wishes be known (e.g. has completed the form on page 148), use her selections. Try to focus on a single theme, such as, "We have no regrets for she lived a full and happy life" — or, "Things we remember about Mother" — or "I am thankful to have known her" . . .

Other suggestions:

- Rather than display cut flowers, you may wish to have potted plants and invite guests, as a remembrance of the deceased, to take them home with them.

- You may wish to pour glasses of her favorite wine or tea, or juice, and ask guests to make a toast to the memory of the deceased.

- Share food, such as her favorite cake or dessert; this is an old tradition which affirms life.

- Join hands in a circle for a moment of silence.

- Decorate with balloons filled with air or helium. "Balloons are filled with breath and like life, have color and are fragile. After the service, please take one or more balloons and when outside, release them to symbolize 'letting go' and saying goodbye."

- Ask guests to respond to the question: "What did knowing _____ add to your life?"

AN EXAMPLE OF A MEMORIAL SERVICE:

Speaker 1: We have gathered together today to remember, with love, our friend, _____, who has died. All living things must die, as we, too, will someday die. It makes us sad that this is so, but nothing lives forever. We light this candle; the light will symbolize for us _____'s life, as we think of how much we love her.

Speaker 2: Although our sadness is great, we also think how glad we are that she lived, and we are thankful that we knew her, for we had happy times together. She was a good friend, a dedicated teacher, an active feminist, mother to _____, partner of (or spouse of) _____, and we loved her. (Use what is appropriate.)

Speaker 1: This is _____'s favorite song. If she were here, she would probably sing or hum along. Please feel free to do likewise. (Have someone sing/or play the song/or use a recording or cassette.)

Speaker 2: _____ would say, "Thanks. That's lovely." This poem (or, these words) seem to have been written about (for) _____. [Or, _____ selected this poem (reading or essay) to be read today.] (Read the selection.)

Speaker 1: _____ was born in _____, the daughter of _____. (Give chronological/or brief history of events as her life is reviewed: or, a brief family history may be presented.)

Speaker 2: Please join in a Responsive Reading. (Select an appropriate reading/prepare copies ahead of time for bereaved.)

Speaker 1: There is no need to lament; let us give thanks for having known _____. Let us share some words about our friend. (Several members of her family and her friends now speak of their remembrances. In the invitation, encourage people to come prepared to say a few words . . .

Speaker 2: (Reads a poem or several sayings.)

Speaker 1: Let us close by —: a) singing (or listening to) _____'s favorite song again (or another favorite song); or b) with another Responsive Reading; or, c) by listening to a recording of an appropriate song, or a person can sing it.

Speaker 2: We have gathered in this place to do honor and praise to the life and memory of _____. We have gathered to offer thanksgiving and gratitude that one such as she has lived among us. We have gathered in celebration of her life, and in doing so, the celebration of death. For life and death are one, even as the river flows to the sea.

Speaker 1: Let us call to memory the dead yet ever-living. Our Sister dwells at peace in the halls of memory whose hallowed treasure it is ours to keep from this day forward.

Speaker 2: Let us depart in peace, and look to the morning, assured that tomorrow the Sun will rise again. Mother Earth gives and Mother Earth takes away. Blessed Be Mother Earth.

Speaker 1: Now for us, the living,
    it is time to leave.
May the love of friends,
    the radiance of memory,
    the hope for an abundant life,
    the power of love
Fill us all with strength and peace
    that we may greet the breaking
    of tomorrow's dawn
With praise and love for one another.

    Blessed Be.
      Go in peace.

Reach high, for stars be hidden in your soul —
Dream deep, for every dream precedes the goal.

If we are ever to enjoy life, now is the time —
Not tomorrow, nor next year, nor in some future life.

— Thomas Dreier

WE BROUGHT NOTHING INTO THIS WORLD, AND
IT IS CERTAIN THAT WE CAN CARRY NOTHING OUT.

If you try to escape from death,

you lose life.

TO ME,
EVERY HOUR OF THE DAY AND NIGHT
IS AN UNSPEAKABLY PERFECT MIRACLE.

Could we see when and where we are to meet again, we would be
more tender when we bid our friends goodbye.

— Ouida

A NATIVE AMERICAN PRAYER

Do not stand at my grave and weep —
I am not there, I do not sleep.
I am a thousand winds that blow.
I am the diamond glint on snow.
I am the sunlight on ripened grain.
I am the gentle autumn rain.
When you wake in the morning hush,
I am the swift, uplifting rush,
Of quiet birds in circling flight.
I am the soft starlight at night.
Do not stand at my grave and weep.
I am not there. I do not sleep.

AN EPITAPH

Here lies a most beautiful woman:
Light of step and heart was she;
I think she was the most beautiful woman
That ever was in this country.
But beauty vanishes; beauty passes;
However rare — rare it be;
And when I crumble, who will remember
This beautiful woman of this country?

—Walter de La Mare, rev.
(1873 - 1956)

A HUSH OF PEACE

A hush of peace — a soundless calm descends;
The struggle of distress; and fierce impatience ends;
Mute music soothes my breast — unuttered harmony.
That I could never dream till Earth was lost to me.

Then dawns the Invisible; the Unseen its truth reveals;
My outward sense is gone, my inward essence feels:
Its wings are almost free — its home, its harbor found,
Measuring the gulf, it stoops and dates the final bound.

—Emily Bronte
From *The Prisoner*

AN UNTIMELY THOUGHT

I wonder what day of the week.
I wonder what month of the year.

T.B. Aldrich (c. 1880)

AS SOMETIMES IN A DEAD ONE'S FACE

As sometimes in a dead one's face,
 To those that watch it move and more,
 A likeness, hardly seen before,
Comes out — to someone of the race.

So, dearest, now thy brows are cold,
 I see thee what thou art, and know
 Thy likensss to the wise below,
Thy kindred with the great of old.

But there is more than I can see,
 And what I see I leave unsaid,
 Nor speak it, knowing Death has made
All darkness beautiful with thee.

—Lord Alfred Tennyson, rev.

ASSUMPTIONS

The people I respect most behave as if they were immortal and as if
society was eternal. Both assumptions are false: both of them must
be accepted as true if we are to go on eating and working and
loving, and are to keep open a few breathing holes for the human
spirit.

— From *Two Cheers for Democracy*
E.M. Forster

AT A CHILD'S GRAVE

My friends: I know how vain it is to gild a grief with words, and yet I wish to take from every grave its fear. Here in this world, where life and death are equal, all should be brave enough to meet what all the dead have met. The future has been filled with fear, stained and polluted by the heartless past. From the wondrous tree of life the buds and blossoms fall with ripened fruit, and in the common bed of earth, patriarchs and babes sleep side by side.

Why should we fear that which will come to all that is? We cannot tell, we do not know, which is the greater blessing — life or death. We cannot say that death is not a good. We do not know whether the grave is the end of this life, or the door of another, or whether the night here is not somewhere else a dawn. Neither can we tell which is the more fortunate — the child dying in its mother's arms, before its lips have learned to form a word, or the person who journeys all the length of life's uneven road, painfully taking the last slow steps with staff and crutch.

Every cradle asks us "Whence?" and every coffin "Whither?" The poor, the uneducated, the religious weeping above their dead, can answer these questions just as well as the rich, the educated or the humanists. The tearful ignorance of the one is as consoling as the learned words of the other, but no person, standing where the horizon of a life has touched a grave, has any right to prophesy a future filled with pain and tears.

It may be that death gives all there is of worth to life. If those we press and strain within our arms could never die, perhaps that love would wither from the earth. It may be that common fate treads from out the paths between our hearts the weeds of selfishness and hate. And I had rather live and love where death reigns, than have eternal life where love is not. Another life is nought, unless we know and love again the ones who love us here.

They who stand with breaking hearts around this little grave, need have no fear. The larger and the nobler faith in all that is, and is to be, tells us that death, even at its worst, is only perfect rest. We know that through the common wants of life — the needs and duties of each hour — their grief will lessen day by day, until at last this grave will be to them a place of rest and peace — almost of joy. There is for them this consolation: The dead do not suffer. If they live again, their lives will surely be as good as ours. We have no fear. We are all children of the same mother, and the same fate awaits us all. We, too, have our religion, and it is this: Help for the living — Hope for the dead.

—Robert Ingersoll
Washington, D.C.
January 8, 1882, rev.

Life is a flame that is always burning itself out,
but it catches fire again every time a child is born.

Be not heavy upon her, O earth: she was not so to thee.

—Martial
Epigrams, Bk.v, epig. 34 (C.A.D. 90)

Her spirit has left her body; night seals her eyes.

—Seneca
Hercules Oetaeus, 1, 841 (C.A.D. 60)

A TOAST

I raise the wine glass
   in loving memory of _____.

I sip its sweet flavor
   affirming life —

> WHICH OUR DELIGHTFUL FRIEND
> HELD SO DEAR.

I offer a toast
   to her memory.

A remarkable woman;
   well-read —

> WITH WIT AND WISDOM:
> WITH ZEST AND ZEAL,
> AND DOGGED DETERMINATION.

She wove the tapestry of her life
   into a beautiful pattern —

> WITH SUNRISE AND SUNSETS
> WITH CHILDREN AND FLOWERS
> WITH TRAVEL AND TRIUMPHS.

I raise the wine glass
   in your memory, _____.

> GO IN PEACE
> OUR BELOVED FRIEND
> KNOWING THAT YOU WERE LOVED
> AND ADMIRED
> BY US
> YOUR FRIENDS.

Blessed Be.

      mb

ATOMS IN THE AIR

Her smile was brighter than morning sunlight
Her laughter healed better than any medicine
Her memory charms us still.

Her sparkling light dimmed and is gone
Yet we cannot grieve more than a moment
For she is all around us
With her smile
Her laughter
Her memory.   mb

Death ends a life, but it does not end a relationship,
which struggles on in the survivor's mind toward
some resolution which it may never find.

We arrive in this world alone, we depart alone;
this time called life . . . was meant to share.

How little we have—time, energy, and treasure—and yet,
how little it takes to make the difference between love and envy, courage and dismay, composure and alarm. We live by
fractions—just a little sign of confidence from someone and
we are braver, just a little understanding and we are more
loving, just a little help to lift the burden of fear and the
world is better.

—Rev. William L. Fox
Universalist National Memorial Church
Washington, D.C.

BEYOND THE SEA OF TIME

So vast can be our universe
So much our eyes can't see,
Our minds can never grasp it all
And hold it eagerly,
Today is such a few short hours
Tomorrow so sublime,
We often fail to see at all
Beyond the sea of time.

Beyond the day we're living in
Into the world unknown,
So little do we realize
How much is not our own,
We cannot measure life it seems
In days or months or years,
For minutes end in nothingness
And doubts bring needless fears.

Beyond the scope of yesterday
Into a sea of blue,
A golden sunset ever there
Where dreams can all come true,
It matters not what day or hour
What's yours or what is mine,
We find that life's an endless thing
Beyond the sea of time.

An unknown bit of earth and sky
That years cannot erase,
A bit of ocean clear and blue
Earth's own bright smiling face,
Was never meant that we should know
Though still tis true and fine,
Our eyes were never meant to look
Beyond the sea of time.

—Author Unknown

BLESS OUR COURAGE

In the midst of life,
   we are in death.

The spirit of our beloved Sister
   dwells in our hearts.
We have the courage, in love,
   to carry forward her memory
     in the lives we now lead.

Mother Earth, receive from us
   the person of _____.

Let the best which was her,
   be renewed in strength in us.
May we now give to others the love
   that we no longer can give to her.
For the lives we lead are now
   her honor and her memorial.

She would bless our courage.

May we have peace.
She would wish it so.

So let it be.
Blessed Be.

               mb

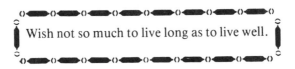

Wish not so much to live long as to live well.

The act of dying is also one of the acts of life.
          —Marcus Aurelius
Meditatio w. Bk. vi, sec. 2 (C.A.D. 174)

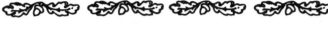

BOUNDARIES

The poet says
You cannot disturb a flower —

WITHOUT TROUBLING A STAR.

The scientist says
There are no sharp boundaries —

BETWEEN WHAT THE HUMAN BEING IS
AND WHAT THE UNIVERSE IS.

Susan Griffin says
We give the grass a name,
and earth a name.
We say grass and earth are separate.
We know this because we can
pull the grass free of the earth
and see its separate roots —

BUT WHEN THE GRASS IS FREE IT DIES.

Blessed Be.   mb

Life doesn't begin in a womb, or end in a grave. Life began billions of years ago on this wondrous green planet. We don't know where it came from, or why, or where it goes from here.

CANDLE LIGHTING

For Seven People

Adapted from "Dear Men and Women," John Hall Wheelock

1. We present this ceremony on or near November 1st as the day after Hallowe'en is the day Roman Catholic and Anglican churches celebrate "All Saints Day." God is glorified for having inspired all those people—known and unknown—who have lived saintly lives. We each have lists of "Our Saints"—individuals whom we admire and love because they have helped or inspired us at various times in our lives. For thousands of years, people observed the Soltice by lighting ceremonial fires. Fire for warmth. Fire for light. Fire to symbolize life and remembering. One of the rituals of the Catholic Church is to light a candle for a person who has died. Today, we will light candles in gratitude and commemoration to a few of the many people we each wish to remember, those people who have loved us, inspired us and who have made significant contributions to our individual lives.

   These are the kinds of people John Hall Wheelock had in mind when he wrote the poem "Dear Men and Women":

   In the quiet before cockcrow when the cricket's
   Mandolin falters, when the light of the past
   Falling from the high stars yet haunts the earth
   And the east quickens, I think of those I love—
   Dear men and women no longer with us.

   I light this candle in memory of _____ .*

2. And not in grief or regret merely but rather
   With a love that is almost joy when I think of them,
   Of whom I am part, as they of me, and through whom
   I am made more wholly one with the pain and the glory,
   The heartbreak at the heart of things.

   I light this candle in memory of _____ .*

3. I have learned it from them at last, who have grown old
   A happy person, that the nature of things is tragic
   And meaningful beyond words, that to have lived
   Even if once only, once and no more,
   Will have been — oh, how truly — worth it.

   I light this candle in memory of _____.*

4. The years go by: March flows into April,
   The sycamore's delicate tracery put on
   Its tender green; April is August soon;
   Autumn, and the raving of insect choirs,
   The thud of apples in moonlight orchards;
   Till winter brings the slant, windy light again
   On shining Manhattan, her towering stone and glass;
   And age deepens — oh, much is taken, but one
   Dearer than all remains, and life is sweet
   Still, to the now enlightened spirit . . .

   I light this candle in memory of _____.*

5. And there they dwell, those ineffable presences,
   Safe beyond time, rescued from death and change,
   Though all be taken, they only shall not be taken —
   Immortal, unaging, unaltered, faithful yet
   To the lost dream world they inhabit.

   I light this candle in memory of _____.*

6. Truly, to me they now may come no more,
   But I to them in reverie and remembrance
   Still may return, in me they still live on;
   In me they shall have their being, till we together
   Darken in the great memory.

   I light this candle in memory of _____.*

7. Dear eyes of delight, dear youthful tresses, foreheads
   Furrowed with age, dear hands of love and care —
   Lying awake at dawn, I remember them,

With a love that is almost joy I remember them:
Lost, and all mine, all mine, forever.

I light this candle in memory of _____.*

PREPARATION

1. Place seven candles in candleholders on a table in front of your audience, with a book of matches.
2. Photocopy script and assign each reader a part. Have readers stand in consecutive order and when not reading, look at the person who *is* reading and *not* down at the script.

*Specify a person and say a few words about the person being commemorated.

When I remember bygone days
I think how evening follows morn;
So many I loved were not yet dead,
So many I loved were not yet born.

—Ogden Nash

CEREMONIAL MOURNING SONG

" . . . things may be going well for you one day, then something happens and you are destroyed. This is the way life is. Remember, it can happen to you, too."

Diegueno: Native American

RESPONSIVE READING

CHOOSE LIFE

Oh, Death, where is your sting?
Oh, Grave, where is your victory?

WHERE IS HOPE AND LOVE AND PEACE?

We all must die,
    and are as water spilt on the ground,
        which cannot be gathered up again.

WE ARE LOOKING FOR HOPE.

Blessed are those who mourn,
    for they shall be comforted.

WE LOOK FOR HOPE AND REACH OUT FOR LOVE.

Blessed are those that weep,
    for they shall know laughter.

WE HAVE HOPE AND WE SEEK LOVE.

Before you is life and death.
    Choose life, that both you and your
        descendants may live.

WE CHOOSE LIFE.   mb

Having chosen life you have found hope,
and you can find love,
and then you shall know peace.

WE CHOOSE LIFE.

Be ever-hopeful.
Keep love in your life,
and know that peace comes from within.

WITH LIFE THERE IS HOPE AND LOVE AND PEACE.

Blessed Be.

mb

Without a heart for loving, living would be the hardest task in life.

WHAT IS LIFE?

In a little while I will be gone from you, my people, and whither I cannot tell. From nowhere we come, into nowhere we go. What is life? It is the flash of a firefly in the night. It is the breath of a buffalo in the winter time. It is the shadow that runs across the grass and loses itself in the sunset.

—Chief Crowfoot
1836 - 1890
Blackfoot Tribe

CLOSING I

I am saddened by death when it comes. In most cases I would like to be able to chase it away, to be able to harken up the magic that would cure all the cancer, prevent all the heart attacks, avert all the accidents and quirks of fate that do in our bodies. But this can't be done. Death comes, and will always come, in its own time and its own way, and none of us will be able to avoid it. To have to die is the price we pay for having been given life in the first place.

That is why it is important to remember the way people like _____, people who are aware of how close they are to death, live. Instead of giving in to fear and depression, though they experience both, they let their awareness of their finitude mobilize rather than *im*mobilize their lives. _____ was able to live well, remarkably well. She fought to stay alive. She wasn't superhuman, though, and the time finally came when no amount of courage or will could sustain her against the ravages of her disease. The time came when, having lived and loved as fully as she could, she moved into her death with dignity, leaving those of us who knew her enriched because of our sharing with her.

Thanks, _____. We won't forget you. Your body has been returned to the elements from which we all come, but inside us there is a part of you that lives on. We promise to give the good that was in you an immortality. We won't forget you.

Dr. David Sammons, rev.
UU Walnut Creek, CA
Original memoralized Bob Forbes

CLOSING II

The body of our loved one has been committed to purifying flame (or to the keeping of Mother Earth who bears us all). Earth to earth, ashes to ashes, dust to dust. We are glad that she lived. We are glad that we saw her face, and felt the glow of her friendship. We cherish the memory of her words, her deeds and her character. In love we will remember her life and the years of companionship and friendship. And as we think of her, let us go in quietness and peace, to live *our* lives in joy and peace and with charity one to another.

> The days are slipping through my fingers
> no matter how hard I hold.

COMMITTAL

Down gently down
Softer to sleep
Than bed at night
Go.

Down gently down
Darker than night
Into the vast greatness
Go.

The earth as Mother, the womb from which all living things are born and to which all return as death, was perhaps the earliest representation of the divine in protohistoric religions.

— "From Mother Goddess to Dishwasher,"
Natural History, February 1973.

CONSOLE MY SOUL

The loveliness of youth —

> SO BRIEF ITS HOURS
> IT LIVES BUT A DAY.

The busy years of maturity —

> THEY, TOO, END
> AND FADE AWAY.

And then old age —

> WHERE DID
> THE TIME GO?

And now death takes you away —

> I WISH
> IT WERE NOT SO.

Console my soul — for _____ lived a long, full life —

> FILLED WITH FAMILY, FRIENDS, AND LOVE.

Console my soul — for _____ lived with faith, not strife —

> WITH FAMILY, FRIENDS AND LOVE.

Springs fresh in Minnesota —

> SUMMERS WARM IN NORTH DAKOTA.

Falls cool in Arizona —

> WINTERS WHITE IN COLORADO.*

*Revise this so that the states (or towns) reflect the life of the deceased.

Console my soul, for _____ lived a long, full life —

     FILLED WITH LOVE
        WITH FAMILY
        AND WITH FRIENDS.

Blessed Be.   mb

For my mother, Hazel Madeline Whiting Gunnerud.

YOU HAVE TOUCHED ME
I HAVE GROWN.

Joy is not in things, it is in us.

If we are to appreciate other people,
   if we are to live with patience,
   gentleness and love,
Let us be about it today,
for life is short.

              —Ernest Morgan

Live each day to the fullest and find joy in all you do.

DAWNING

Stand high upon a mountain, as day is born anew...
Kneel down and smell a flower, still fresh with morning dew...
Run beside the river, so wild, and free, and blue,
Reach out your hand, and catch the wind, it will not wait for you...
Walk slowly through the meadow, till closing of the day...
Reach out and touch the sunset, before it slips away.

Neli Herring

This instant is the only time there is.

We regret more things we didn't do than things we did do.

— Aesop

Seek not the life of the immortals;
but enjoy to the full
the resources
that are within thy reach.

—Pindar

Even if the doctor does not give you a year, even if s/he hesitates about a month, make one brave push and see what can be accomplished in a week.

—Robert Louis Stevenson

DEAR LOVELY DEATH

Dear lovely Death
That taketh all things under wing —
Never to kill —
Only to change
Into some other thing
This suffering flesh,
To make it either more or less,
But not again the same —
Dear lovely Death,
Change is thy other name.

Langston Hughes

Look to this day, for it is life. For yesterday is but a dream, and tomorrow only a vision. But today, well lived, makes each yesterday a dream of happiness, and every tomorrow a vision of hope.

—Sanskrit proverb and credo of the hospice movement

DEATH

I cry, I am afflicted
We must leave the beautiful flowers

Let's enjoy ourselves for a while
Let's sing

We will depart forever
We are destroyed in our dwelling place

Pain and anger
Knowing never again can they be born
Never again young on this earth

Only a brief time with them
Then nevermore with them
Nevermore enjoy them
Nevermore know them

Ancient Mexico/Nahuatl

DEATH

Death is our enemy. Death is the denial of life. Death is grim and
implacable. Death is the final act of our lives.

DEATH: GOOD DYING

Those who know and can deeply accept the ephemeral nature of their own life are the best companions for those who, as we say, are leaving this life.

Over the years I have gradually learned to let the dying teach me to die and in teaching me to die they have taught me to live. I have learned from them how human it is to deny death, to be angry at death, to bargain with death, to be depressed at the thought of death and to accept death. The miracle is the high levels at which the acceptance may come to pass in a far ranging play of courage and faith and thanksgiving, and love, prayer, and song.

> On the day when death will knock at thy door
> What wilt thou offer to him?
>> Oh, I will set before my guest the full
>> vessel of my life.
>> I will never let him go with empty hands.
>> All the sweet vintage of all my autumn
>> days and summer nights, all the earnings
>> and gleanings of my busy life will I
>> place before him at the close of my days
>> when death will knock at my door.
>
> (Rabindranath Tagore)

—Harry B. Scholefield

A long life may not be good enough but a good life is long enough.
—Benjamin Franklin

DEATH OF A CHILD

Beneath the canopy of the infinite heavens
   and in this place of peace,
     set apart from the world's stresses and griefs,

       WE PRAY FOR AN UNDERSTANDING
       OF THE AGE-LONG MYSTERY OF DEATH
       AND MYSTERY OF LIFE.

Into the friendly earth
   which has served as a final resting-place
   of innumerable bodies
   of those who have lived before us
   and left the stage,

       WE COMMIT THE BODY OF THIS CHILD,
       HER COMING WELCOMED WITH READY LOVE,
       HER EARTHLY SPAN SO BRIEF,
       HER DEPARTURE SO SUDDEN.

Like a nascent particle she arrived,
   she flashed across our vision,
   she was gone,

       AND WE ARE LEFT
       WITH BUT A PHOTOGRAPHIC TRACE
       IN THE CLOUDED CHAMBER
       OF OUR MINDS.

But through the eons of time,
   from which we glean the story
   of our world,

       OUR LIVES ALSO
       ARE BUT A MOMENTARY FLASH,
       GIVING SCARCELY TIME TO ASK:
       WHY ARE WE HERE
       AND WHITHER BOUND?

Let us then be not overly concerned
  with the length of our lives.

        LET US RATHER TAKE THOUGHT
        FOR THE QUALITY.

Since it has been given to us
  to live under the guidance of our own dedication
  to some noble purpose,

        MAY THE DEATH OF THIS LITTLE ONE
        RECALL US TO OUR OWN DESTINY
        AND STRENGTHEN US
        IN OUR LOYAL COMMITMENT
        TO THOSE WHO REMAIN WITH US.

As we sometimes think of her
  and what she might have become,

        MAY WE THINK OF OURSELVES
        AND THE KIND OF LIVES
        SHE WOULD HAVE WISHED US
        TO LIVE FOR HER.

        THUS MAY HER LIFE,
        THOUGH BRIEF,
        BE AN ETERNAL INFLUENCE
        UPON THOSE
        WHOM SHE DID NOT LINGER
        TO MEET.

Adapted from Elma A. Robinson, mb

If there is anything better than to be loved, it is loving.

DEATH OF A DEAR FRIEND

Next to our own death, the most traumatic calamity
    is the death of a dear friend.
We are moved to shock and to tears.
We weep,
We pray.
We are angry —
We accuse fate, but we cannot alter it.
We mourn —
    Knowing that the comfort of having a friend may be taken away,
    but not that of having one.
We have lost what we had, yet we retain what is lost.
We learn — we endure
    And we resolve to treasure the warmth of friendship.
Let us therefore enjoy our friends while we have them.

DEATH OF A FRIEND

O people of the whole world!
You have lost a friend.
One who loved and respected the people
    of the whole world,
and the places where they lived —

She respected your traditions and customs:
She knew your hungers, your sorrows,
    your songs.
She wanted to help you live fully,
To use the Earth wisely,
To rejoice in living.

Her name is _____.

DEDICATION

From the gardens
Of my friends' thought,
I have gathered
The most beautiful flowers.

With thanksgiving and much care,
I shall replant them
  so that others
May enjoy the fragrance
When we will be only
  a memory.

—J. Zecchitella

DIRGE WITHOUT MUSIC

I am not resigned to the shutting away of loving hearts
  in the hard ground.
So it is, and so it will be, for so it has been, time out of mind:
Into the darkness they go, the wise and the lovely. Crowned
With lilies and with laurel they go; but I am not resigned.

Lovers and thinkers, into the earth with you.
Be one with the dull, the indiscriminate dust.
A fragment of what you felt, of what you knew,
A formula, a phrase remains, — but the best is lost.

The answers quick and keen, the honest look, the laughter,
  the love, —
They are gone. They are gone to feed the roses. Elegant and curled
Is the blossom. Fragrant is the blossom. I know.
  But I do not approve.
More precious was the light in your eyes
  than all the roses in the world.

Down, down, down into the darkness of the grave
Gently they go, the beautiful, the tender, the kind;
Quietly they go, the intelligent, the witty, the brave.
I know. But I do not approve. And I am not resigned.

—Edna St. Vincent Millay

DO NOT LET ME DIE

Do not let me die!
Farmers at your raking,
When the sun is high...
Do not let me die.

Read me, do not let me die.
Search the fading letters finding
Steadfast in the broken binding
All that once was I.

> —Edna St. Vincent Millay
> *The Poet and His Book*

EPITAPH

Heap not on this mound
    Roses that she loved so well;
Why bewilder her with roses,
    That she cannot see or smell?

> —Edna St. Vincent Millay

EPITAPH

Weep not, ye mourners, for the dead,
But in this hope your spirits soar,
That ye can say of those ye mourn,
They are not lost, but gone before.

—Alexander Pope (c. 1731)

EPITAPH

"Never in Silence."

EPITAPH

"And now for something
completely different."

EPITAPH

"Forget the epitaph — live!"

EPITAPH

"Here lies an atheist —
all dressed up and no place to go."

THE EXHORTATION OF THE DAWN

Look to this day!
For it is life, the very life of life.
In its brief course lie all the verities and
realities of your existence:
The bliss of growth,
The glory of action,
The splendor of beauty;
For yesterday is but a dream,
And tomorrow only a vision;
But today, well lived, makes every yesterday
a dream of happiness.
And every tomorrow a vision of hope.
Look well, therefore, to this day.

— From the SANSKRIT, circa 1200 B.C.E.

How long a life is, is of little consequence. What counts is what we do with the days we have. Do we move toward what we are by seeking? Or do we deny what we are by refusing to accept it?

May you live all the days of your life.
—Jonathan Swift

Two thousand years ago, Seneca commented that "death sometimes a punishment, often a gift, and for many a favor."

FACING DEATH

Through a willingness to risk the unknown,
to venture forth into unfamiliar territory —

I CAN UNDERTAKE THE SEARCH
FOR MY INNER SELF —
THE ULTIMATE GOAL OF GROWTH.

FOR 'LIFE IS RISK, OR IT IS NOTHING AT ALL.'

Through reaching out and committing myself
to exchange feelings with those I care about —

I CAN BEGIN TO TRANSCEND MY INDIVIDUAL
EXISTENCE
BECOMING AT ONE WITH MYSELF AND WITH
OTHERS.

FOR OTHERS ARE THE REFLECTION OF MYSELF.

And through a lifetime of such commitment,

I CAN FACE MY FINAL END WITH PEACE AND
JOY —
KNOWING THAT I HAVE LIVED MY LIFE WELL.

I HAVE TOUCHED AND BEEN TOUCHED
I HAVE GIVEN AND I HAVE RECEIVED.

I AM AT PEACE.

Blessed Be.

—Inspired by Elisabeth Kubler-Ross'
Death: The Final Stage of Growth
and a quote of Emma Goldman's, mb

FAREWELL TO A SISTER

The song is done
The eastern sun rises
The stars repose in the darkened sky.
>   OUR SISTER NO LONGER HEARS THE BIRDS
>   FEELS THE WARMTH OF THE SUN
>   PONDERS THE VAST EXPANSE OF SPACE.

The bell has tolled for thee
The candle has been spent
The flower that bloomed so brightly has faded.
>   OUR SISTER NO LONGER JOINS OUR CIRCLE
>   HOLDS OUR HAND
>   SMILES OR CRIES OR
>   CALLS US ON THE TELEPHONE.

We bid you farewell,
>   REST IN PEACE.

The time we shared together —
>   WILL BE REMEMBERED WITHIN OUR HEARTS
>   FOR YOU ARE PART OF US.

Dear Sister, 'the moving finger, having writ, moves on' —
>   WE MOURN
>   WE GRIEVE
>   WE SORROW.

The earth moves
We move on —
>   KNOWING WE ARE BORN
>   IN OUR MOTHER'S PAIN
>   AND WE PERISH IN OUR OWN.

Knowing that time —
>   IS OUR MOST PRECIOUS GIFT.

Farewell,
>   FAREWELL, SISTER.

Blessed Be.   mb

FLOWER OF HOPE

I had rather think of those I have loved and lost as having returned to earth, as having become a part of the elemental wealth of the world, I would rather dream of them as unconscious dust; I would rather dream of them as laughing in the stream, floating in the clouds, bursting in light upon the shores of other worlds; I would rather think of them as the lost visions of a forgotten night, than to have even the faintest fear . . . But as for me, I will leave the dead where nature leaves them. Whatever flower of hope springs in my heart I will cherish; I will give it breath of sighs and rain of tears.

—R.G. Ingersoll, *The House of Death*

FOR THAT TIME OF SORROW

I share with you the agony of your grief,
>The anguish of your heart finds echo in my own.
>I know I cannot enter all you feel
>Nor bear with you the burden of your pain;
I can but offer what my love does give:
>The strength of caring,
>The warmth of one who seeks to understand
>The silent storm-swept barrenness of so great a loss.
This I do in quiet ways,
>That on your lonely path
>You may not walk alone.

—Howard Thurman

FRAIL BARQUE

The waters that Old Age must cross
Are cold and deep and dark
And only they that enter know
How faint the spark
That flickers in the breast;
How dim eyes look to farther shore
And long for promised rest.
But flickering flame is fanned
By breath of love divine
And faithful hearts look up
Where stars of hope still shine.
Life's siren song no longer charms
But Hope and Faith and Love sustain
And Death is kind.

—Antoinette Craig Matthews

To be seventy years young is something far more cheerful
and hopeful than to be forty years old.

I don't see living having to do with any special goal or end. It seems
to me living has to do with just that — living. It's a process. We are
either living and using those things that are around us to work with
today, or we're not.

"FREEDOM"

When I die and
Leave behind this earth
I love,
These trees
This sky
The everpounding sea,
The yearly hope of spring,
      Cry not for me
        Rejoice!
My soul has wings and in its
      "Freedom"
      "Sings!"

—J. Danziger

MAY YOU LIVE AS LONG AS YOU LIKE
AND
LIKE AS LONG AS YOU LIVE

As you add years to life
add life to years.

I am not afraid of tomorrow for I have seen yesterday and I love today.

FRIEND

Green be the turf above thee,
  Friend of my better days!
None knew thee but to love thee,
  Nor named thee but to praise.

—Fitz-Greene Hallek, 1820

GONE

The light of her young life went down,
  As sinks behind the hill
The glory of a setting star, —
  Clear, suddenly, and still.

As pure and sweet, her fair brow seemed
  Eternal as the sky,
And like the brook's low song, her voice, —
  A sound which could not die.

The blessing of her quiet life
  Fell on us like the dew;
And good thoughts, where her footsteps pressed,
  Like fairy blossoms grew.

There seems a shadow on the day,
  Her smile no longer cheers,
A dimness on the stars of night,
  Like eyes that look through tears.

—John G. Whittier
(shortened)

GOOD-BYE

Life is but weak if we waste it in weeping:
So, she has left you, — she would, soon or late, —
Death from our lives takes all in her keeping,
Nothing we do can our sorrow abate.

Love, be it ever so deep and entire,
Asks that we strive for the end that she sought:
Catch the tossed torch! Take up the fire!
Light up the lectern and teach as she taught.

Giving is receiving.

. . . who-we-are is rooted in our kinship with the natural. The water of life flows through our tissues, and we are nourished, watered, fed, sustained, and ultimately return everything in our bodies to the world around us.

—Elizabeth Dodson Gray
Green Paradise Lost

GRANDMOTHER

O, softly waves the silver hair
　　From off that aged brow!
That crown of glory worn so long,
　　A fitting crown is now.

Fold reverently the weary hands
　　That toiled so long and well;
And, while your tears of sorrow fall,
　　Let sweet thanksgivings swell.

That life-work, stretching o'er long years,
　　A varied web has been;
With silver strands by sorrow wrought,
　　And sunny gleams between.

These silver hairs stole slowly on,
　　Like flakes of falling snow,
That wrap the green earth lovingly
　　When autumn breezes blow.

Each silver hair, each wrinkle there,
　　Records some good deed done;
Some flower she cast along the way,
　　Some spark from love's bright sun.

How bright she always made her home!
　　It seemed as if the floor
Was always flecked with spots of sun,
　　And barred with brightness o'er.

The very falling of her step
　　Made music as she went;
A loving song was on her lip,
　　The song of full content.

And now, in later years, her word
　　Has been a blessed thing
In many home, where glad she saw
　　Her children's children spring.

O, gently fold the weary hands
   That toiled so long and well;
The spirit rose to angel bands,
   When off earth's mantle fell.

She's safe within death's mystery,
   Wherever it may be;
O, pray that thus such rest may come,
   Dear heart, to thee and me!

                — Anonymous

THE GREAT GIFT OF LIFE

I want to say something to all of you
   who have become a part
   of the fabric of my life.

When the time
   of our particular sunset comes
Our belongings, our accomplishments
   won't really matter a great deal.

But the clarity and care
   with which we have loved others
   will speak with vitality
   of the great gift of life
   we have been for each other.

                —G. Norbet

GRIEF WORK: THE HEALING PROCESS

Some feelings that normally arise when someone we care about dies are:

1) **Denial.** "This is not happening. There must be some mistake!"

2) **Physical distress.** One can experience a wide variety of digestive, respiratory, hormonal, and cardiovascular ailments — tight throat, shortness of breath, lack of energy, inner tension or pain. Physical distress can result in handwringing, aimless walking and other muscular hyperactivity, including hair or clothes-pulling. One teenage girl I know thoroughly cleaned the entire house when she heard her mother had died.

3) **Emotional release.** A flood of tears. A scream. A realization of loss which is the beginning of healing.

4) **Being out of touch with reality.** One can feel as though what is happening is unreal and feel like an outsider looking on. One can feel emotionally distant from other people and pre-occupied with the image or memory of the deceased. Shock and numbness are especially acute in the case of sudden loss.

5) **Guilt.** Guilt feelings are common symptoms of grief. Thoughts of one's shortcomings and all the wrong things one did in relation to the deceased and all the good things one failed to do can become overwhelming. Guilt is especially apt to arise when there were unresolved conflicts, and when a person died after a long illness and the survivor(s) feel relief that the ordeal is over; or, when one has worked through their grief and then feels guilty because they have nothing left to grieve at the time of death.

6) **Hostility.** Another common grief response is feeling cold and irritable toward others. One doesn't want to be bothered by others during one's time of bereavement and is critical and easily upset with those who offer comfort.

7) **Anger.** "Why did you leave me? I'm all alone now! How dare you!" Anger may be directed at the deceased for dying, or at anyone who might be blamed. Anger is an emotion frequently difficult to face and to share.

8) **A sense of loss.** As one's normal living pattern is disrupted, restlessness takes over and significant parts of one's life lose significance. One feels isolated and lonely. It becomes almost impossible to carry on routine activities and one becomes depressed and obsessed with the subject of life and death.

9) **Depression.** Sadness and grief can develop into depression, even to thoughts of suicide. Even though it's difficult to do, should one become unkempt, let things go and develop a "Why try?" attitude, *seek help*: Talk to a medical doctor or a professional counselor, find a support group, contact a local Center for Living With Dying agency, talk to a Humanist counselor or a Unitarian Universalist minister. Physical exercise is one of the best ways to overcome depression so take a brisk walk every day, swim, run . . .

10) **Need to talk.** Go ahead and express feelings, share memories, and seek meaning in life — the deceased's life, your life, and life in general.

11) **Obsessive concern with health and safety.** After a loved one dies, one's health and the health and safety of family members may become an obsessive concern. To allay fears regarding health, have a medical check-up. Take precautions and then relax about safety measures. Try to divert your attention elsewhere.

12) **Panic.** Feeling unable to cope with an unknown future, survivors sometimes feel there is something wrong with them and, feeling overcome, panic and do irrational things.

13) **Taking on characteristics of the deceased.** A final symptom of grief is to attempt doing things "because she would want it this way."

14) **Taking positive action.** It is positive action when you work to avoid similar deaths for others. It is healing to reach out to persons similarly bereaved. When you complete projects started by the deceased you are now ready to reach out for new relationships and new experiences. When you take positive actions, you are ready to go on with your life.

Through "Grief Work" the bereaved work through feelings of pain and loss and anger* in order to move ahead with their lives. Acknowledge that your loved one has died and will never return. Face reality. Know that you are not responsible for the death and verbalize and communicate these feelings to another person. Get on with your life.

Trying to avoid memories and deny the pain of bereavement is unhealthy. Don't be ashamed of your feelings. Cry and let out the depth of how badly you feel. Grief, guilt, anger, and hostility are normal responses to loss. Letting feelings out is part of the grief process which allows pain that goes with loss of a loved one to heal. Realize that your life was made richer by having the opportunity of knowing and sharing your life with the person who has died. Then, you will begin to live in the present and plan for the future, instead of being bound to the past and your memories. Then, you will find yourself living more fully than ever.

Relationships are not quite the same after the death of a loved one. Within a family, a "new" set of relationships emerge. When a beloved friend dies, a part of us dies, too. We have shared a person's life and we are custodians of these memories. It is time to affirm values and remove any sense of guilt. It is a time to express love and solidarity and the profound meaning of life.

When a loved one dies, it is a time to know how precious our relationships are and to re-live the memories of the earlier years. We have lost part of ourselves so it is normal to experience loneliness and insecurity. It is a time for family and friends to give encouragement and strength. It is a time to hug one another.

*A bereaved person can get stuck in some stage of grief. Seek professional help should you stay longer than three months in a stage of grief.

HOLY GROUND

We meet on holy ground,
For that place is holy where we meet one another.
Where lives touch,
Where love moves,
Where hope stirs,
There is holy ground.

How strong our need is for one another:
Our silent beckoning to our neighbors,
Our invitations to share life and death together,
Our welcome into the lives of those we meet,
And their welcome into our own.

We meet on holy ground,
Brought into being as life encounters life,
As personal histories merge into the communal story,
As we take on the pride and pain of our companions,
As separate selves become community.

Some day or other the last hour will strike also for me.

—Tacitus
Dialogues de Oratoribus, Sec. 13 (c. A.D. 85) quoting an unknown
author.

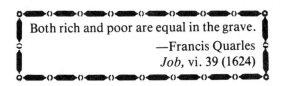

Both rich and poor are equal in the grave.
—Francis Quarles
Job, vi. 39 (1624)

HOME-GOING

The rugged Scandinavians of old spoke of death as "Home-going." So the snow flowers go home, when they melt and flow to the sea, as myriads of rejoicing living creatures — daily, hourly — perhaps every moment, are cradled in the arms of death. All the merry dwellers of the earth and trees and streams, and all the myriad swarms in the air — called life by the sunbeam of a summer morning — go home to the loving arms of Mother Earth.

— from John Muir, adapted by W. Tabler

My country is the world, and my religion is to do good.

— Thomas Paine

I'll speak to you a word of hope and share your heavy load.

—W.F. Jabusch
From *In My Name*

All say "How hard it is to die" — a strange complaint from people who have had to live. Pity is for the living, envy for the dead.

—Mark Twain

HUMAN HANDS ARE FOR TOUCHING

The touching of hands is an ancient
   ritual written deep in us.
As greeting it welcomes us into the
   intimacy of others.
As farewell it assures us we shall be
   missed.
In bereavement it speaks of our
   common hurt.
In love it is silent sure sharing needing
   no words.

The touching of hands in a human
   circle welcomes all to its warmth.
In steep places it gives and receives
   strength in climbing.

The trembling touching of hands is a
   cry for help none may ignore.
The tentative touching of hands is an
   invitation to reach out to include.

The touching of hands is a small thing.
It is the sharing of life with life.

                —Rev. Richard S. Gilbert
                      Rochester

HUMANKIND IS ONE

It is the same at the end
  as it was in the beginning —

> WE COME OUT OF THE WOMB OF THE MOTHER
> TO OPEN OUR EYES,
> AND WE RETURN TO THE GRAVE
> WITH OUR EYES CLOSED.

The world that gave us forth
  in magnificent motherhood —

> RECEIVES US BACK TO HER
> ALL-EMBRACING BOSOM.

The world is the rejoicing mother
  and the grieving woman —

> GIVING BIRTH AND SUFFERING THE DEATH
> OF ALL HER BELOVED OFFSPRING.

Humankind is one —

> WHEN AS INFANTS
> WE ARE HELD TO THE BREAST.

Humankind is one —

> WHEN AS CORPSES
> WE ARE GIVEN BACK TO THE FLAMES
> AND THE DUST.

If we would learn it —

> HUMANKIND IS ALSO ONE
> DURING THE FEW YEARS
> OF BREATH WE CALL LIFE.

When will we live as one humanity?

EVEN AS WE ARE NOW BORN ONE,
AND DIE ONE?

— Adapted from **This World, My Home**
Kenneth L. Patton, mb

Do not squander time, for that is the stuff life is made of.

— B. Franklin

To be what we are, and to become what we are capable of becoming, is the only end of life.

—Robert Louis Stevenson

Be not afraid of life. Believe that life is worth living, and your belief will help create the fact.

— William James

Far happier are the dead, methinks, than they
Who look for death, and fear it every day.

—Wm. Cowper
On Invalids (1782)

The following is a letter written by Nadine Stair at age 85:

IF I HAD MY LIFE TO LIVE OVER

If I had my life to live over, I'd dare to make more mistakes next time. I'd relax; I'd limber up. I would be sillier than I have been this trip. I would take fewer things seriously. I would take more chances. I would climb more mountains and swim more rivers. I would eat more ice cream and less beans. I would perhaps have more actual troubles, but I'd have fewer imaginary ones.

You see, I'm one of those people who lived sensibly and sanely hour after hour, day after day. Oh, I had my moments, and if I had it to do over again, I'd have more of them. In fact, I'd try to have nothing else. Just moments, one after the other, instead of living so many years ahead of each day. I've been one of those persons who never goes anywhere without a thermometer, a hot water bottle, a raincoat and a parachute. If I had it to do over again, I would travel lighter than I have.

If I had my life to live over again, I would start barefoot earlier in the spring and stay that way later in the fall. I would go to more dances; I would ride more merry-go-rounds. I would pick more daisies.

YEARS WRINKLE THE SKIN,
BUT TO GIVE UP ENTHUSIASM WRINKLES THE SOUL.
— Samuel Ullman

IF THE PEOPLE LIVE THEIR LIVES

If the people live their lives
As if it were a song for singing out of light
Provides the music for the stars
To be dancing circles in the night.

IF THERE IS NEVER AN END

We pause in reverence before all intangible things—
that eyes see not, nor ears can detect—
that hands can never touch—
that space can not hold—
and time can not measure.

There is never an end to our yearning to
know the unknown—
after all our labor at learning.
There is never an end to our trying the untried—
after all our failures in striving.

Fling wide the windows, O my soul!
The bright beams of morning are warm.

—Sophia Lyon Fahs

IN CELEBRATION

We meet —

> TO CELEBRATE THE LIFE OF _____.
> TO EXPRESS WITH LOVE
> HOW MUCH SHE MEANT TO US.

We meet —

> TO HUG ONE ANOTHER.
> TO AFFIRM LIFE
> TO AFFIRM THAT _____
> WAS IMPORTANT TO US.

We join together —

> TO EXPRESS OUR LOVE.
> TO SHARE OUR LOSS
> TO CELEBRATE HER LIFE.

Blessed Be.

mb

TRUE FRIENDSHIP COMES WHEN SILENCE BETWEEN
TWO PEOPLE IS 'COMFORTABLE.'

Life is too short *not* to improve relationships
with the people you live with —

INSTRUCTIONS...

When I have moved beyond you in the adventure of life,
   gather in some pleasant place
   and there remember me
   with spoken words, old and new.

Let a tear fall if you will,
   but let a smile come quickly
   for I have loved the laughter of life.

Do not linger too long with your solemnities,
   go eat and drink and talk
   and when you can —
      follow a woodland trail
      climb a high mountain
      sleep beneath the stars
      swim in a cold river
      chew the thoughts of some book which
        challenges your soul
      use your hands some bright day
        to make a thing of beauty
        or to lift someone's heavy load.

Though you mention not my name,
   though no thought of me crosses your mind —
   I shall be with you
   for these have been realities of life to me.

And when you face some crisis with anguish —
   when you walk alone with courage
   when you choose your paths of right
   when you give yourself in love
I shall be very close to you.

I have followed the valleys,
   I have climbed the heights of life.

                — Arnold Crompton

I SHALL NOT CARE

When I am dead and over me bright April
    Shakes out her rain-drenched hair,
Though you should lean above me broken-hearted,
    I shall not care.

I shall have peace, as leafy trees are peaceful
    When rain bends down the bough;
And I shall be more silent and cold hearted
    Than you are now.

—Sara Teasdale

I SHALL NOT LIVE IN VAIN

If I can stop one heart from breaking,
I shall not live in vain;
If I can ease one life the aching,
Or cool one pain,
Or help one fainting robin
Unto his nest again,
I shall not live in vain.

—Emily Dickinson

JOB'S PATIENCE

Quicksilver column fell — so did the rain
Upon the just and unjust all alike.
We are to have Job's patience, not complain,
We are to take deaths when and as they strike.
Job's cattle are destroyed on vale and hill,
His herds and goods are blasted in the night;
In neutral Nature there is neither good nor ill:
His prayers did not avail to heal his plight.

Where can we turn our life to dignify?
Are we people, or just clods?
The hand that placed the Pleiades on high
Saves not a people from the wrathful rod.
Nor God nor Job has answered to my call:

Why should young friends be taken from us all?

—for Dr. Ann Snee
Aged 30

Give all that you have to the here and now.

When you face the void left by your loss, sorrow and grief can
seem, at least for the moment, almost too much to bear.

KINDLING THE FLAME OF REMEMBERING

For My Mother
(Name — Dates)

O Mother Earth, Blessed One,
As I kindle the light — the flame of memory —
Help me to realize mother's death
So that I may realize
Her life and
   her love.

Re-align my daughter spirit
   with the spirit of _____, my mother.
Help me to see her face in my dreams —
Find hints of her noble nature,
Her pride of self
Her distinctive voice
And her quiet sensitivity.

O Mother Earth, Blessed One,
   as I strike the match
   to the candle of remembering,
I ask you to send the light of mother's soul
   into my heart —
Warming me with her flame,
Her love comforting me.

"Cease your tears, my child,
  You buried my bones
  You mourned me in secret
  You wept,
  You grieved.
  — Now
Set these aside.

"We are one, you and I,
  Mother and Daughter,
  Bound up in the bonds of living.

"There is no death, my daughter,
  No ending.
  There is only change.
  All existence is a circle —
  birth, dying, birth, dying, birth, dying.
  The flowers of Spring,
  The fruits of Harvest,
  The dried leaves of Winter warming
    the seeds for the garden.

"All, we all — (*list several relatives, friends,
  honored ones who have died*)
  are part of
  Earth,
  Sea,
  Sun,
  Cloud.
  Moving
  Changing
  Crying
  Birthing
  Blooming.

"My daughter,
  I am alive because
  You have kindled the flame of remembering,
  You have chosen to share
  Our love with loved ones."

O Mother Earth, Blessed One,
  May the light of love,
  And the light of happiness
  Live on forever
  In the love that each of us
  Shares with one another.

May such love be handed down,
Generation unto generation.

— Marylou Hadditt

KINDNESS

I shall pass through this world but once
Any good therefore that I can do
Or any kindness that I can show to any human being
Let me do it now.
Let me not defer it nor neglect it,
for I shall not pass this way again.

—Stephen Qrellet
New Jersey Quaker
Died 1855

There are two important dates in each of our lives,
only one of these is known, our *birth*-day.
The second date is our inevitable death, which is unknown.

Know the true value of time. Snatch, seize, and enjoy every moment of it.

—Lord Chesterfield

Here hath been dawning another blue day: think, wilt thou let it slip useless away? — Thomas Carlyle

LAMENT FOR BION

Ay me! when the mallows and the fresh green parsley and the springing crumpted anise perish in the garden, they live yet another and grow another year; but we that are so tall and strong and wise, soon as ever we be dead, unhearing here in a hole of the earth sleep we both sound and long a sleep that is without end.

Mochus 1 98 (c. 150 B.C.E.)

Oh death! where is thy sting?
Oh grave! where is thy victory?

A perfect climate
Without good will does not make
A perfect people.

Nature in the raw
Shows no divine attitude
Of benevolence.

—from Africa

The dead are dead.
—Euripides

Alcestic, 1.541.(438 B.C.E.)

> Death tracketh everything living and catcheth it in the end.
> —Sappho
> *To Her Pupils.* Frag 118 (c 610 B.C.)

Our body dies, but we do not die. To some degree, each life changes society and influences other lives. The life of Sappho, 2600 years dead, has influenced our lives. And yes, our influence will be upon life yet unborn. Each life, brief as it is, makes a momentary light which can last a long, long time.

TO LESBIA

My Lesbia, let us love and live,
And to the wind, my Lesbia, give
Each cold restraint, each boding fear
Of age and all her saws severe.
Yon sun now posting to the main
Will set, — but 'tis to rise again;
But we, when once our mortal light
Is set, must sleep in endless night.
Then come, with whom along I'll live,
A thousand kisses take and give!
Another thousand! — to the store
Add hundreds — then a thousand more!
And when they to a million mount,
Let confusion take the account, —
That you, the number never knowing,
May continue still bestowing —
That I for joys may never pine,
Which never can again be mine!

— Catullus
(Translated by Samuel T. Coleridge)

You may forget but

Let me tell you
This: Someone in
some future time
will think of us.

— Sappho, 580 B.C.

★LOVE
  ★LOVE ISN'T LOVE UNTIL YOU GIVE IT AWAY.
   ★LOVE IS THE GREATEST GIFT WE CAN GIVE
   EACH OTHER.
      ★LOVE DOES NOT MEAN LOOKING AT EACH
      OTHER, BUT LOOKING TOGETHER IN
      THE SAME DIRECTION.
         ★LOVE IS A BRICK WALL PUT UP
         PIECE BY PIECE —
         EACH BRICK
         BUILDING AND
         STRENGTHENING
            THE TOTAL WALL.

Without a heart for loving, living would be the hardest task in life.

THOSE WHO LOVE DEEPLY NEVER GROW OLD.
THEY MAY DIE OF OLD AGE,
BUT THEY DIE YOUNG.

Parting is all we know of heaven, and all we need of hell.

— Emily Dickinson

If you love somebody, let them know.

MARGARITAE SORORI

A late lark twitters from the quiet skies:
And from the west,
Where the sun, its day's work ended,
Lingers as in content,
There falls on the old, gray city
An influence luminous and serene,
A shining peace.

The smoke ascends
In a rosy-and-golden haze. The spires
Shine and are changed. In the valley
Shadows rise. The lark sings on. The sun,
Closing its benediction,
Sinks, and the darkening air
Thrills with a sense of the triumphing night —
Night with its train of stars
And its great gift of sleep.

So be my passing!
My task accomplish'd and the long day done,
My wages taken and in my heart
Some late lark singing,
Let me be gather'd to the quiet west,
The sundown splendid and serene,
Death.

                                    —W.E. Henley

The greatest tragedy of any death is to reach the end without having really lived at all.
                                    —Leo Buscaglia

MEDITATION XVII

John Donne, rev.

The passing bell doth call us all.
The bell doth toll for those who think it doth.

Who casts not up their eye to the sun
    when it rises? But who takes off their
    eye from a comet when it breaks out?
Who bends not their ear to any bell which
    upon any occasion rings? But who can
    remove it from that bell which is passing
    a piece of themselves out of this
    world?
No one is an island entire of itself; every
    person is a part of the main.
If a clod be washed away by the sea,
    Europe is the less, as well as if a
    promontory were, as well as if a manor
    of their friend's or of thine own were.
Any person's death diminishes me, because
    I am involved in humankind, and therefore
    never send to know for whom the bell tolls;
It tolls for thee.

Death is the line that marks the end of all.

—Horace
Epistles, Bk. i, epis. xvi, 1 79 (B.C. 20)

MEMOIR

Abrasive
Loud
Uppity

> SHE NEVER ACCEPTED THE ROLE
> OF SUBSERVIENT WOMAN.

Nurturing
Caring
Teaching

> SHE TOUCHED THE LIVES
> OF ALL SHE MET.

Creative
Articulate
Always growing

> SHE READ A THOUSAND BOOKS
> AND SAW A THOUSAND FILMS.

Organizing
Raising consciousness'
Radical

> SHE SPOKE HER MIND, CHIPS
> FALLING WHERE THEY MAY.

Atheist
Socialist
Humanist*

> SHE KNEW LIFE WAS FRAGILE
> LIFE WAS SHORT
> AND
> WE BETTER GET ON WITH IT.

Blessed Be.   mb

*Feel free to change labels, but keep them when read
at *my* memorial.

MEMORIAL

No epitaph inscribed on the most elaborate of monuments will ever be read by the one for whom it was written even if the lettering is of burnished gold. The only memorial that can make any difference is the personal growth stimulated by the life and the passing of the one who is gone.

—Rev. Daniel Panger
UU Minister, San Mateo, CA

Life is not a having and a getting, but a being and a becoming.
—Matthew Arnold

The minute you know that you are not afraid to die, is the minute you begin to know how to live.
—H.F. White

MORITURUS

If I could have
   Two things in one:
The peace of the grave,
   And the light of the sun;

My hands across
   My thin breast-bone,
But aware of the moss
   Invading the stone,

Aware of the flight
   Of the golden flicker
With his wing to the light;
   To hear him nicker

And drum with his bill
   On the rotted willow;
Snug and still
   On a grey pillow

Deep in the clay
   Where digging is hard,
Out of the way, —
   The blue shard

Of a broken platter —
   If I might be
Insensate matter
   With sensate me

Sitting within,
   Harking and prying,
I might begin
   To dicker with dying.

For the body at best
   Is a bundle of aches,
Longing for rest;
   It cries when it wakes

"Alas, 'tis light!"
   At set of sun
"Alas, 'tis night,
   And nothing done!"

Death, however,
   Is a spongy wall,
Is a sticky river,
   Is nothing at all.

Summon the weeper,
   Wail and sing;
Call him Reaper,
   Angel, King;

Call him Evil
   Drunk to the lees,
Monster, Devil, —
   He is less than these.

Call him Thief,
    The Maggot in the Cheese,
The Canker in the Leaf, —
    He is less than these.

Dusk without sound,
    Where the spirit by pain
Uncoiled, is wound
    To spring again;

The mind enmeshed
    Laid straight in repose,
And the body refreshed
    By feeding the rose, —

These are but visions;
    These would be
The grave's derisions,
    Could the grave see.

Here is the wish
    Of one that died
Like a beached fish
    On the ebb of the tide:

That he might wait
    Till the tide came back,
To see if a crate,
    Or a bottle, or a black

Boot, or an oar,
    Or an orange peel
Be washed ashore . . .
    About his heel

The sand slips;
    The last he hears
From the world's lips
    Is the sand in his ears.

What thing is little? —
    The aphis hid
In a house of spittle?
    The hinge of the lid

Of the spider's eye
    At the spider's birth?
"Greater am I
    By the earth's girth

"Than Mighty Death!"
    All creatures cry
That can summon breath; —
    And speak no lie.

For He is nothing;
    He is less
Than Echo answering
    "Nothingness!" —

Less than the heat
  Of the furthest star
To the ripening wheat;
  Less by far,

When all the lipping
  Is said and sung,
Than the sweat dripping
  From a dog's tongue.

This being so,
  And I being such,
I would liever go
  On a cripple's crutch,

Lopped and felled;
  Liever be dependent
On a chair propelled
  By a surly attendant

With a foul breath,
  And be spooned my food,
Than go with Death
  Where nothing good,

Not even the thrust
  Of the summer gnat,
Consoles the dust
  For being that.

Needy, lonely,
  Stitched by pain,
Left with only
  The drip of the rain

Out of all I had;
  The books of the wise,
Badly read
  By other eyes,

Lewdly bawled
  At my closing ear;
Hated, called
  A lingerer here; —

Withstanding Death
  Till Life be gone,
I shall treasure my breath,
  I shall linger on.

I shall bolt my door
  With a bolt and a cable;
I shall block my door
  With a bureau and a table;

With all my might
  My door shall be barred.
I shall put up a fight,
  I shall take it hard.

With his hand on my mouth
  He shall drag me forth,
Shrieking to the south
  And clutching at the north.

—Edna St. Vincent Millay

MOTHER

Mother has left us —

    GENTLY SHE DEPARTED
    SLEEPING SOUNDLY
    SLOWLY DOWN THE STAIRS OF LIFE.

A mother's love —

    WE SHALL NOT SEE AGAIN
    FOR OUR MOTHER IS GONE.

For the second time —

    THE UMBILICAL CORD IS CUT
    AND WE ARE SEPARATED FROM OUR MOTHER.

Gone are the ties —

    THAT BIND
    ONE GENERATION TO ANOTHER.

And we know —

    WE ARE THE NEXT IN LINE
    TO FACE THE DYING OF THE LIGHT.

Gone are her days —

    LET GO AND SAY GOODBYE.

Her brows are smooth —

    HER HOPES AND FEARS SET FREE.

Let us rejoice —

> THAT WE HAD MOTHER
> AS LONG AS WE DID.

For this precious gift —

> WE GIVE THANKS.

Mother has left us —

> WE CRY OUT, FRIGHTENED
> THE TEAR DROPS FALL.

Our voices tremble —

> WE HAVE LOST HER
> TO THE COMMON DESTINY
> OF ALL EARTHLY THINGS.

We bear our grief —

> MOTHER HAS LEFT US
> OUR MOTHER IS GONE.

mb

For my mother, Hazel Madeline Whiting Gunnerud.

Yea, though I walk through the valley of the shadow of death, I will fear no evil.

—Old Testament, Psalms, xxiii, 4 (c. 350 B.C.)

MOTHER EARTH

Mourn not our Sister —

> WHO HAS RETURNED TO MOTHER EARTH.

In the cool earth she lies —

> DUST UNTO DUST.

The sweet earth that mothers all who die —

> AS ALL WE MUST.

Mourn not our Sister —

> WHO SPOKE OUT AGAINST GREED
> IN HER DEFENSE OF MOTHER EARTH.

Mourn not our Sister —

> WHO LIVED HER LIFE FULL
> NOT COWED AND MEEK.

Mourn not our Sister —

> WHO SAW THE WRONGS AND
> FOUGHT THE GOOD FIGHT.

In the cool earth she lies —

> DUST UNTO DUST.

The sweet earth, mother to us all —

> FOR DIE WE MUST.

Blessed Be.

mb

MY BEST FRIEND

Right up to the end
She was my friend.

She was my very dearest friend
One on whom I could always depend.

I was stronger, knowing that she
Would always take time to talk to me.

She was my friend through thick and thin
Regardless of the shape I was in.

We laughed and ate a lot of food
Gave each other massages and swam in the nude.

Seasons came and seasons went
My time with her was the best I spent.

I will not sorrow, for she
and my memories keep me company.

Right up to the end
She was my friend.

My best friend.

mb

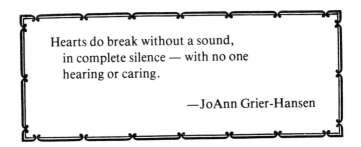

Hearts do break without a sound,
   in complete silence — with no one
   hearing or caring.

—JoAnn Grier-Hansen

MY FRIEND

Because of her
And her special qualities
I am a better person.

Her sincerity
Her optimism
Her generosity
Gave me strength.

She was my anchor.
She helped me over the rough spots
— through the difficult times —
I owe her a lot.

Her joy reverberated like a melody
Which echoes still within me,
She gave life a special glow.
She was my friend.

mb

SISTERHOOD IS POWERFUL.

MY SEVENTY-FIFTH BIRTHDAY

I strove with none, for none was worth my strife.
   Nature I loved and, next to Nature, Art:
I warmed both hands before the fire of life;
   It sinks, and I am ready to depart.

                       —W.S. Landor

NATURE'S SPHERE

The city's smog cannot subdue the trees;
Petunias grow beside the noisy way:
The birds and bees still sound their harmonies;
The thunder and the raindrops have their say —
Beside the concrete lies our fertile soil
Prepared to furnish us with divers goods;
It takes a little faith, a little toil
To coax from mud some grains or other foods;

We humans, too, are part of Nature's sphere —
We're from the earth, and to it we return;
We have days that oppress us, times that cheer
Some things we get with no cost, some we earn —
_____ lived so, with humor and with zest;
We can live so — at least can do our best.

           — F.O.S. for Mae Spencer Schultz
                d. August 3, 1975

NOTHING IS HERE FOR GRIEF OR TEARS

Her later years crawled on;
Her way grew steep;
Her heart beat fast;
Her road grew dark;
As night came on,
And all was hush.

Far back, the horizon is aglow;
Children play and laughter fills the air,
All frozen now in that long ago,
When for _____, the morning sun and time began.

Between that sound and this silence,
Her eyes grew dim,
Her hearing failed,
The road curves up,
And the muscles tire,
And breath 'comes short,
And the heart beats fast,
And the night comes on,
And all is hush.

                              — Ward Tabler

NOW

God came softly in the night
Touched her gently, finger light
Smoothed the anguish from her brow,
And gently whispered — Now.

NOW THAT YOU'RE GONE

As your memory begins to fade,
I think how much I miss you —
And I feel so alone.

I cry until I'm numbed,
And then I feel —
    the loneliness
    the fear
    the anger
    the pain
    the desolation.

I hope I heal soon;
I miss you so.

Our friends are still here —
    they give me comfort,
But they don't feel my loss —
    or know my sadness.

I know healing will take time.
I know I will smile again
    and laugh, and sing —
I know that.

But for now —
    I am not whole.
I feel so alone —
    and as your memory begins to fade,
I think how much I miss you —
    now that you're gone.

                          mb

O DEATH

O Death divine, at whose recall
Returneth all
To fade in thy embrace,
Gather thy children to thy bosom starred,
Free us from time, from number, and from space,
And give us back the rest that life hath marred.

—Alfred de Vigny

OF SHADOWS AND DUST

Sometimes I don't glance at the sky
To spot where the sun is, and how the clouds roll by.
Sometimes I don't observe the resulting play of shadows,
And when I don't pause to glance and reflect,
I fleetingly re-experience the shadowless high noon of youth,
Our lives are but an interface between sunrise and sunset,
Dramatically emerging out of shadows and moving into shadows.

The stuff of life is time, dust and direction,
Time is the most personal of things,
Expressive and unending in youth,
Compressed and finite in age.
As the stuff of our lives are spent, time itself accelerates,
Then dwindles away as the final grains drop through the hour glass.

I, _____ of the dust, dreaming my dreamless dreams,
Embrace the cool comforting shadowless night,
Foreshadowing, by the play of the elementals, where I long to be,
For this is the way to high noon.

—Ted Ruhig
(To the memory of Helen Himley)

THE OLD WOMAN'S FUNERAL

I saw an aged woman upon her bier;
   Her hair was thin and white, and on her brow
A record of the cares of many a year, —
   Cares that were ended and forgotten now.
And there was sadness round, and faces bowed,
And men's tears fell fast, and children wailed aloud.

Then rose another older woman, and said,
   In faltering accents to that weeping train;
"Why mourn ye that our aged friend is dead?
   Ye are not sad to see the gathered grain,
Nor when their mellow fruit the orchards cast,
Nor when the yellow woods let fall the ripened mast.

"Ye sigh not when the sun, its course fulfilled, —
   Its glorious course, rejoicing earth and sky, —
In the soft evening, when the winds are stilled,
   Sinks where the islands of refreshment lie,
And leaves the smile of its departure spread
O'er the warm-colored heaven and ruddy mountain-head.

"Why, weep ye then for her, who, having won
   The bound of one's appointed years, at last,
Life's blessings all enjoyed, life's labors done,
   Serenely to her final rest has passed;
While the soft memory of her virtues yet
Lingers, like twilight hues when the bright sun is set?

"Her youth was innocent; her riper age
   Marked with some act of goodness every day;
And, watched by eyes that loved her, calm and sage,
   Faded her late declining years away:
Meekly she gave her being up, and went
To share the rest that waits a life well spent.

"And I am glad that she has lived thus long,
   And glad that she has gone to her reward;
Nor can I deem that nature did her wrong,
   Softly to disengage the vital cord;
For, when her hand grew palsied, and her eye
Dark with the mists of age, it was her time to die."

— William Cullen Bryant
(shortened with reversed gender)

From ON THE NATURE OF THINGS, BOOK III

No single thing abides; but all things flow.
Fragment to fragment clings — the things thus grow
   Until we know and name them. By degrees
They melt, and are no more the things we know.

Globed from the atoms falling slow or swift
I see the suns, I see the systems lift
   Their forms; and even the systems and the suns
Shall go back slowly to the eternal drift.

Thou too, oh earth — thine empires, lands, and seas —
Least, with thy stars, of all the galaxies,
   Globed from the drift like these, like these thou too
Shalt go. Thou art going, hour by hour, like these.

Nothing abides. Thy seas in delicate haze
Go off; those mooned sands forsake their place;
   And where they are, shall other seas in turn
Mow with their scythes of whiteness other bays . . .

The seeds that once were we take flight and fly,
Winnowed to earth, or whirled along the sky,
   Not lost but disunited. Life lives on.
It is the lives, the lives, the lives, that die.

They go beyond recapture and recall,
Lost in the all-indissoluble All: —
   Gone like the rainbow from the fountain's foam,
Gone like the spindrift shuddering down the squall.

Flakes of the water, on the waters cease!
Soul of the body, melt and sleep like these.
   Atoms to Atoms — weariness to rest —
Ashes to ashes — hopes and fears to peace!

O Science, lift aloud thy voice that stills
The pulse of fear, and through the conscience thrills —
   Thrills through the conscience with the news of peace —
How beautiful thy feet are on the hills!

—Lucretius
(Translated by W.H. Mallock)

OUR HOUR TO GRIEVE

You are gone —
AND A PART OF ME HAS PASSED AWAY.
For our lives mingled
WITH SHARED MEMORIES OF WORK AND PLAY.

Time will dull the pain —
LIFE WILL GO ON
And when I die —
OUR MEMORIES WILL BE GONE.

Our link in the cycle of life —
OUR BRIEF JOURNEY ON PLANET EARTH —
Our part in the great chain of being —
IS DEATH AND BIRTH / DEATH AND BIRTH.

All living things are fleeting —
RICH AND POOR / SAINTS AND SINNERS.
No life lives forever —
THE GRIM REAPER ALLOWS NO WINNERS.

We are born and we die —
LIFE SOWS / DEATH REAPS.
The day begins — and it ends —
THE SUN HAS SET / THE SKY WEEPS.

In this, our hour of grief —
WE LAY WREATHS WHERE SHE LIES.
We cannot choose —
OUR HOUR TO DIE.

You are gone —
IT IS OUR HOUR TO GRIEVE.

Blessed Be.   mb

Death is the natural end of life.

OUR WORLD

Our world is cyclical.

    —We are born.
    —We live.
    —We die.

Our world is interrelated.

    —For each act
        there is a reaction.
    —For each birth
        a death.

Our world is beautiful.

    —the trees and the flowers.
    —the rivers and the oceans.
    —the cities and the towers.

Our world is temporary.

    —We cry.
    —We laugh.
    —We die.

These are the ways of our world.

Blessed Be Our World.

                      mb

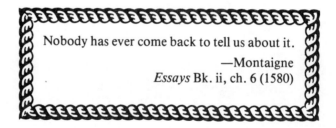

Nobody has ever come back to tell us about it.
              —Montaigne
        Essays Bk. ii, ch. 6 (1580)

PASS'N THROUGH

Pass'n through, pass'n through,
Sometimes happy, sometimes blue,
Glad that I ran into you
Tell the people that you saw me pass'n through.

What we have once enjoyed we can never lose again
A sunset, a mountain, or the sea
We will ever love their beauty, hold the vision in our hearts,
Our memories will always hold the key.

Whomever we have loved becomes a part of us.
A loved one is truly never lost.
They still laugh and work and play, we remember them that way.
Love cannot lose whatever be the cost.

— adapted by Ward and Barbara Tabler
from a poem by Helen Keller

Worrying about what happens when you die is like worrying about what happens to your lap when you stand up.
—Zen Koan

I can only die once and then it'll be over.
—Patricia Wentworth
Pursuit of a Parcel (1942)

POEM FOR THE LIVING

When I am dead,
Cry for me a little.
Think of me sometimes,
But not too much.
It is not good for you
Or your wife or your husband
Or your children
To allow your thoughts to dwell
Too long on the dead.
Think of me now and again
As I was in life.
At some moment which it is pleasant to recall.
But not for long.
Leave me in peace
As I shall leave you, too, in peace.
While you live,
Let your thoughts be with the living.

—Theodora Kroeber

Remember, today is the first day of the rest of your life.

The awareness of death is the source of zest for life and of our impulse to create not only works of art, but civilizations as well.

—Rollo May

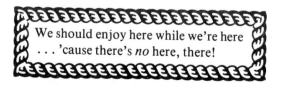
We should enjoy here while we're here
. . . 'cause there's *no* here, there!

PONDER THIS THING

Out of the stars in their flight,
  out of the dust of eternity
  have we come.

> STARDUST AND SUNLIGHT
> MINGLED THROUGH TIME AND SPACE.

Time out of time, before time,
  in the vastness of space,
      earth spun to orbit the sun.

> EARTH WARMED BY SUNLIGHT,
> LIT BY SUNLIGHT,
> KINDLED BY SUNLIGHT,
> EARTH GAVE BIRTH TO LIFE.

Ponder this thing in your heart;
  ponder with awe; out of the sea trembled life,
  up from the darkness to light,
  rising to walk and to fly.

> PONDER THIS THING IN YOUR HEART:
> LIFE FROM THE SEA,
> WARMED BY THE SUN,
> WASHED BY THE RAIN:
> EYES TO BEHOLD,
> THROATS TO SING,
> MATES TO LOVE.

This is the wonder of time — this is the marvel of space —
  out of the stars swung the earth; out of the earth
  emerged life; out of life sprang love.

> PONDER THIS THING.

Inspired by *Out of the Stars,*
Robert T. Weston, mb

Blessed Be.

PROOF OF LIFE

Death is not the enemy; living in constant fear of it is.

The way we choose to live and the depth of our feelings, our ability to love and be loved and to take in all the colors of the world around us—these determine the worth and true extent of whatever time we have. The clock keeps ticking away. Our job is to put as much meaning as possible into the intervals between the ticks. A minute can open out into a vast realm in which all our senses, finely attuned, can come into full and splendid play—or those same senses can be shut down, imparting nothing to our years except numbers.

What makes time so valuable is that it is convertible into nourishing memory. Memory is where the proof of life is stored. It offers material for stocktaking and provides clues about where our lives are going.

—Norman Cousins

Life is a gift
for which we are grateful.
We gather in community
to celebrate the wonder
and mystery of that
great gift.

We are left behind to invent a life without _____.
Death sparks our creative resources.
Death teaches us to live.

PSALM

We are brought to the dust;
> TO DUST WE MUST RETURN.

A thousand years are
A day that has passed
As a watch in the night.
> WE ARE CONSIGNED TO SLEEP;

Like grass, we are fresh
In the morning, in the morning
We sprout, blossom forth;
> IN THE EVENING
> WE WITHER AND FADE.

Our days decline
> AND END IN A SIGH:

Destined for seventy,
With strength for eighty —
> MOST OF US TOIL AND TRAVAIL,
> SOON TO PASS AS WE FAIL.

Let's then value our days.
> HALLOWING EACH WITH GRACE —

As a trust bestowed upon us,
> ACQUIRING A HEART FULL OF WISDOM
> AND LOVE FOR THE LIVING OF EARTH.

Through all the days though we suffer
> AND ALL THE YEARS THOUGH WE SORROW,
> REJOICE AND BE GLAD ALWAYS,

For the precious gift give thanks:
> LIVE FOR THE GOOD EACH DAY.

> — An adaptation, mb

RAGE

All life dies. We are mortal. We live our lives in the shadow of death. We resent the ever-present shadow of death, we cry out against the injustice of Mother Nature.

"Do not go gentle into that good night,
old age should burn and rave at close of day;
Rage, rage against the dying of the light."

—Dylan Thomas

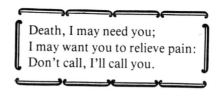

Death, I may need you;
I may want you to relieve pain:
Don't call, I'll call you.

It is a truism that as one gets older,
more of one's friends die.

Each hour slowly steers us nearer death.
—Columbanus
Carmen Monostichon l. 21 (c. A.D. 600)

It all comes to this, while we scurry and worry, up creeps death upon us.

—Plautus
Pseudolus, l. 684. (c. 195 B.C.)

REFLECTION ON TIME

We are here to celebrate the life of _____
    who blessed our lives.
We are grateful for having shared
    our lives with her.
We affirm life knowing that life and death
    are one.
We reflect on time.
Our days are few.
Our lives are part of the secrets
    of creation.
Our birth and our death
    are the pulsations of eternity.

                          mb

---

*Fear not that thy life shall come
to an end, but rather fear that it
shall never have a beginning.*
    —John Henry Newman

If the world is not to last forever, it seems to make no difference
whether its time is to be counted in millions or billions of years;
what matters is that there is an end.

                          —Freya Stark

REMEMBER ME

The young child no longer speaks.
   Yet, in the still of the day,
      We hear her voice
        and her footsteps.
She is saying —
   "I was too young to die.
      Remember me."

                          mb

Lucky to die before you implore death to come.
—Pubillius Syrus
Sententiae No. 354 (c.43 B.C.)

SLEEP WELL, SISTER

She was a feminist —
    A FRIEND OF THE OPPRESSED.

She believed —
    THAT EQUALITY CAME FIRST,
    PEACE ON EARTH WAS THE GOAL.
    REASON WAS IMPERATIVE,
    AND LOVE CONQUERED ALL.

She added to our joy —
    SHE LOVED LIFE
    AND SHE MADE THE WORLD
    A BETTER PLACE.

She worked for the common good —
    SHE FILLED HER LIFE
    AND THERE ARE NO REGRETS.

She was our tender comrade —
    AND WE LOVED HER.

Bless her, Mother Earth —
    WARM HER DEEP.
    OUR SADNESS
    OUR TEARS
    STAIN OUR CHEEKS.

Sleep well, my Sister —
    SLEEP WELL.

Blessed Be.   mb

"Looking at death is dying."
    — Emily Dickinson

SO BE IT

Some say there is a silence
    in the forest
When wind and rain prune the
     boughs of ash and oak,
And persons hear it not,
    nor care. So be it.

But let the great Sequoia fall,
    and all are made aware.
The willows weep.
For here, the breath of life
    and span of years
      the girth of trunk
       and depth of root
Make tremors and echoes
    in the minds
    and hearts
    and lives
of us all. So be it.

Anonymous

If one were given five minutes' warning before sudden death, five minutes to say what it had all meant to us, every telephone booth would be occupied by people trying to call up other people to stammer that they loved them.

—Christopher Morley

SONG

Say that air remembers lark —

    SAY THAT SEA REMEMBERS SHARK.

Say that earth remembers mole —

    SAY THAT FIRE REMEMBERS COAL.

Who knows? Who knows?

    TIME GOES ITS WAY
    WHATEVER WE SAY.

Say that hand remembers right —

    SAY THAT EYE REMEMBERS LIGHT.

Say that mind remembers truth —

    SAY THAT LOVE REMEMBERS YOUTH.

Who knows? Who knows?

    TIME STEALS AWAY
    WHATEVER WE SAY.

— From Carl Seaburg, **The Voyage**
and other poems, 1961

There is no cure for birth and death save to enjoy the interval.
—George Santayana

SONG

She's somewhere in the sunlight strong,
Her tears are in the falling rain,
She calls me in the wind's soft song.
And with the flowers she comes again.

Yon bird is but her messenger,
The moon is but her silver car;
Yea! sun and moon are sent by her,
And every wistful waiting star.

—Richard LeGallienne

Another year? What of it? Do we live and grow by the hour? Do we not in a moment sometimes age years through an experience? Do we not in a year sometimes move not a step further than where we stood before?

—Anais Nin

I think of death as some delightful journey
That I shall take when all my tasks are done.

—Ella Wheeler Wilcox
The Journey (1901)

The whole of life is the process of giving birth to ourselves; indeed we should be fully born when we die.

—Erich Fromm

SONNET

Like treasure lost at sea, her loveliness
Lies buried now: unchanged, inviolate,
Beyond all sounding, glassy depths possess
That beauty; naught has perished small or great.
Far from this surface world of weeks and days,
The coming summer or the winter's cold,
Ineffably her own, a thousand ways
Rest in the dark of understanding, hold
Color and light against that other death
Oblivion. Sunk in silence they await
The moving tide of memory at whose breath
Waters divide above our doomed estate;
Her look, her laugh, her step upon the stair,
Leaping to life, incomparably fair.

—Elizabeth Morrow

SONNET

And you as well must die, beloved dust,
And all your beauty stand you in no stead;
This flawless, vital hand, this perfect head,
This body of flame and steel, before the gust
Of Death, or under his autumnal frost,
Shall be as any leaf, be no less dead
Than the first leaf that fell, — this wonder fled,
Altered, estranged, disintegrated, lost.
Nor shall my love avail you in your hour.
In spite of all my love, you will arise
Upon that day and wander down the air
Obscurely as the unattended flower,
It mattering not how beautiful you were,
Or how beloved above all else that dies.

—Edna St. Vincent Millay

All who live must die, and none who die can renew their life on earth.

—Kaibara Ekken
Ten Kun (Ten Precepts) Bk. i (1710)

SOUNDLESS CALM

A hush of peace — a soundless calm descends;
The struggle of distress; and fierce impatience ends;
Mute music soothes my breast — unuttered harmony.
That I could never dream till Earth was lost to me.

Then dawns the Invisible; the Unseen its truth reveals;
My outward sense is gone, my inward essence feels:
Its wings are almost free — its home, its harbor found,
Measuring the gulf, it stoops and dates the final bound.

— From **The Prisoner**
Emily Bronte

The gravesite's finality never fails to elicit blocked tears.
—Erica Jong
Parachutes & Kisses (1984)

SPIRIT OF LIFE

We meet here in the presence of death to do homage to the Spirit of Life. It would behoove us to make this hour Love's Hour and these simple memorial rites Love's Confessional. For it is a tribute to Love that we come to offer today.

Our voices may be the voices of grief, but the language after which grief gropes is the language of Love. And we who gather here come in Love's name to express, for those whose lives have not had the visible presence of Love, a calm and abiding trust in Love's immortality and consecrating power.

None of us can ever escape sadness. Each of us bear our burdens and, in turn, bid our loved ones farewell. Each of us must suffer that sad farewell when loved ones die; and each, in turn, must take that final journey into the dark.

Bitter is the sorrow of bereavement, yet when a loved one passes, remember then the blessing we have received: rejoice that even for so brief a period our life has been enriched and deepened beyond the power of anything to destroy, for when beauty and love touch our hearts something eternal has been created.

In the Spirit of Life we designate this hour to be Love's Hour.

—Robert Terry Weston, rev.

To die would be an awfully big adventure.
—J.M. Barrie
Peter Pan Act iii (1904)

SPRING

If I should die (and die I must), please
    let it be in spring
When I, and life up-budding shall be one
And green and lovely things shall blend with all
    I was
And all I hope to be.
The chemistry
Of miracle within the heart of love and
    life abundant
Shall be mine, and I shall pluck the
    star-dust and shall know
The mystery within the blade
And sing the wind's song in the softness of
    the flowered glade.
April is the time for parting, not because all
    nature's tears
Presage the blooming time of May
But joyous should be death and its adventure
As the night gives way to day.

        —George C. Whitney

TAKE DEATH FOR GRANTED

Take death for granted. It is a good thing. The world could not
move on without it. Live with that particular reckoning behind
you. You will grow old much more cheerfully, if you are willing to
die when the time comes.

        —A. Powell Davies

THEORY OF LIFE

You ask me my theory of life. It is represented by the word will . . .
Life is short, even for those of us who live a long time, and we must
live for the few who know and appreciate us, who judge and
absolve us, and for whom we have affection and indulgence. We
ought to hate very rarely, as it is too fatiguing, remain indifferent a
great deal, forgive often, and never forget.

—Sarah Bernhardt
The Daily Telegraph
London, 28 March 1923

Life is but vain:
  a little love,
a little hate
  and then — good day!

Life is but brief:
  a little hope,
a little dream —
  and then — good night!

THERE IS A SEASON

Like the seasons,
  We are —
    Spring
    Summer
    Autumn
    Winter.

Like all creatures,
  We are —
    Infant
    Child
    Adolescent
    Adult.

Like our Sisters,
  We are —
    Girl
    Maiden
    Woman
    Crone.

For each,
    there is a Season.
For each,
    there is a time to be born,
      and
        for each,
          there is a time to die.

                                        mb

THIS BOOK

This book, when I am dead, will be
A little faint perfume of me ...
I do not write it to survive
My mortal self, but, being alive
And full of curious thoughts today,
It pleases me, somehow, to say,
"This book when I am dead will be
A little faint perfume of me."

—Edna St. Vincent Millay
Journal

TO INEZ MILHOLLAND

Read in Washington, November eighteenth, 1923, at the unveiling
of a statue of three leaders in the cause of Equal Rights for Women

Upon this marble bust that is not I
Lay the round, formal wreath that is not fame;
But in the forum of my silenced cry
Root ye the living tree whose sap is flame.
I, that was proud and valiant, am no more; —
Save as a dream that wanders wide and late,
Save as a wind that rattles the stout door,
Troubling the ashes in the sheltered grate.
The stone will perish; I shall be twice dust,
Only my standard on a taken hill
Can cheat the mildew and red-brown rust
And make immortal my adventurous will.
Even now the silk is tugging at the staff;
Take up the song; forget the epitaph.

—Edna St. Vincent Millay

THIS DAY

From starburst
born,
this vast yet tiny earth
formed, and changed,
and formed anew —
through time beyond belief,
to reach
this day.

And now this spinning earth —
moving, and turning, with the universe,
in its ancient way —
seems almost to pause
like a solstice
on this day.

Yet still,
the spinning earth
creates and destroys
and creates again —
the form, the life,
beginning and ending,
unending:
to reach this day,
to go beyond
this day.

—Mary Heath-Walter

'TIS THE LAST ROSE OF SUMMER

'Tis the last rose of summer,
Left blooming alone;
All her lovely companions
Are faded and gone;
No flower of her kindred
No rosebud is nigh,
To reflect back her blushes,
Or give sigh for sigh.

I'll not leave thee, thou lone one,
To pine on the stem;
Since the lovely are sleeping,
Go sleep thou with them;
Thus kindly I scatter
Thy leaves o'er the bed
Where thy mates of the garden
Lie scentless and dead.

So soon may I follow,
When friendships decay,
And from love's shining circle
The gems drop away;
When true hearts lie withered
And fond ones have flown,
Oh, who would inhabit
This bleak world alone.

—Thomas Moore
Irish Air *

*Thomas Moore, the great Irish lyric poet, did for Irish folk songs
what Burns did for those of his native land. "The Last Rose of
Summer" is among his most famous songs, having achieved great
popularity through its interpolation into the ever popular and
beautiful opera "Martha" by Flotow, to whom the authorship of
the song is sometimes erroneously attributed. The air is an ancient
one, called the "Groves of Blarney," which in turn was taken from
a more ancient Celtic melody.*

THOUGHTS ON MY MOTHER'S FUNERAL

People have asked me about my mother's funeral, about how things went and how I feel. Here are some feelings that have to do with the death of someone close and what can mess up those feelings.

The first things that can upset one's feelings is a minister who believes that what matters is repeating what is in his little black book, rather than establishing a relationship with the family of the person who has died. The minister who presided at my Episcopal mother's funeral never bothered to call or to find out anything about the person to be buried. Yet, during the funeral service he had the gall to boast of the long relationship he had with us and of the love he felt for his flock. I doubt if he understood the effect such an insincere comment had on us. It felt like a slap in the face and made us glad we were not members of his church.

Experiences like this remind me of how much better it is to *not* have a Book of Common Prayer or fixed rituals because we then have to become personally involved with a family if we are to know what needs to be said and done. As a result, though it means a lot more thought and work, we end up with a positive service that feels appropriate to the people involved rather than the sad experience my mother's funeral turned out to be. Each time I am forced to endure an orthodox ritual like that one I come away more sure than ever about the meaning and value of religious humanism.

The other bad thing that happened had nothing to do with the minister. It had to do with the fact that no one had a good cry. It was as though a woman had passed out of life without it affecting anyone. I do not want to lay the blame on the members of my family for this. My mother had been alone, and often sick, for a long time. Her own somber mood was, I am sure, a part of the reason for the unemotional response of people to her death. But I felt horrible listening to all the chit chat and the conversations going on as though no one had died. I finally had to go for a walk by myself so I could have my cry. I knew of no other good way to say goodbye to the woman who had given me birth.

So, when the time next comes to deal with death in our families, let us not let the minister get away with being phony or remote, and let us not forget to shed a tear or two.

—Dr. David Sammons
Mt. Diablo Unitarian
Universalist Church

WARM SUMMER SUN
Warm summer sun, shine kindly here;
Warm western wind, blow softly here;
Green sod above, lie light, lie light —
Good-night, dear heart, good-night, good-night.
— For his daughter's gravestone
Robert Richardson
(adapted by Mark Twain)

WE ARE LEFT BEHIND

We are left behind to invent a life no longer with us.
Death sparks our creative resources.
Death teaches us to live.

WEB OF ENERGY

Only in us do the dead live.
Water flows downhill through us.
The sun cools in our bones.
We are joined with all living
in one singing web of energy.
In us live the dead who made us.

A CLOSING RESPONSIVE READING

WE REMEMBER OUR FRIEND

In this, our hour of grief —

WE COMMIT THE BODY OF OUR BELOVED FRIEND
TO MOTHER EARTH
WHO WILL ONE DAY
WELCOME US ALL.

We are glad that _____ lived —

THAT WE KNEW HER
SHARED HER FRIENDSHIP
AND WALKED PART OF
OUR LIFE WITH HER.

We deeply cherish the memory of _____

HER WORDS
HER SMILES
HER DEEDS.

With respect —

WE BID OUR FRIEND FAREWELL.

In love —

WE REMEMBER HER COMPANIONSHIP
HER KINDLY WAYS.

We remember our friend —

AND WE GO IN QUIETNESS
TO LIVE IN SISTERHOOD
ONE WITH THE OTHER.

Blessed Be.   mb

WE REMEMBER OUR SISTER

We shall never again hear the laughter of our friend —

> NOTHING, IN TRUTH,
> CAN REPLACE OUR COMPANION,
> OUR SISTER.

Nothing can match the treasure of our common memories —

> — OF CONVERSATIONS
> — OF TRIALS ENDURED TOGETHER
> — OF QUARRELS AND RECONCILIATIONS
> — OF PROJECTS AND QUIET TIMES
> — OF MARCHES AND MEETINGS.

We shall never again see her —

> SHE IS GONE.
> DEATH IS ABSOLUTE.

But our memories will live as long as we live —
And as long as each of us lives —

> WE WILL REMEMBER OUR FRIEND
> — OUR COMPANION
> — OUR SISTER.

Blessed Be.   mb

WHAT NEEDS TO BE DONE
WNHEN SOMEONE CLOSE TO YOU DIES:
DECISIONS AND ARRANGEMENTS

View of Death:

In our culture we tend to avoid the subject of death. Death is a normal and necessary part of life. Although we affirm life and its possibilities, grief and sadness arise in response to a loss through death. Our feelings surface and we seek ways of dealing with them. To prepare ourselves for the death of someone close to us, it is often helpful to think through issues which might arise around our own death.

When we let our wishes be known, there is less chance that those who survive will give in to pressures of the moment and allow funeral directors or the conventions and beliefs of others dictate our memorial service. To avoid being memorialized in a completely inappropriate way, write down your wishes. Be very clear so that your immediate family know exactly how you wish to be remembered.*

Ask those close to you to write down *their* wishes because when a loved one dies, decisions and arrangements *must* be made. (See ''My Wishes,'' pp. 148 - 150.)

Basic Options

1. Memorial service after body has been cremated, removed to a medical school, or buried.

2. Funeral in the presence of the body—open or closed casket—followed by removal of the body to a medical school, crematorium, or cemetery.

3. Grave site burial only.

*Be aware that your next of kin chooses how to dispose of your body and they can arrange any type of funeral/memorial service they wish.

DECISIONS AND ARRANGEMENTS:

Funeral Society or Mortuary

1) Contact a funeral society* or a mortuary to make arrangements for the disposition of the body, but never give up your autonomy to them. State laws vary, but bodies need *not* be embalmed; Federal Trade Commission rules prohibit embalming without permission.**

It is advisable to decide whether you prefer the services of a funeral society or a mortuary before you die and make arrangements accordingly. If you have difficulty in finding a local funeral society or an appropriate mortuary, telephone your local Unitarian Universalist church or fellowship, or your local American Humanist Association.

It is okay to telephone several mortuaries to compare prices and services.***

Funeral societies are much less costly than mortuaries and provide most services. It is wise to join a funeral society *now* so that they know your wishes.

*Sometimes called Memorial Society/Neptune Society/Bay Area Funeral Society/People's Memorial Association of Seattle/etc. Write for a *free* list of "Memorial Societies in U.S. and Canada" from Continental Association of Funeral and Memorial Societies, 2001 S Street, N.W., Suite 530, Washington, D.C. 20009.

**Some states have laws requiring embalming under certain circumstances, such as length of time between death and burial, availability of refrigeration, etc.

***Funeral directors are often skilled merchandisers who downplay their cheaper (less profitable) merchandise. Don't buy into a pitch such as the one given my mother when Grandpa Ben died: "I'm sure you don't want your father buried in this inexpensive casket." For objectivity, get someone *not* emotionally involved to go along to select a casket and make arrangements. Services should be simple and inexpensive and it is entirely proper to ask about prices. FTC rules require funeral directors to provide price information on the phone and an itemized price list.

Autopsy

2) To grant a request to perform an autopsy to obtain medical knowledge is a humanitarian idea. Even in death a person can be helpful and increase knowledge. If death occurred by suicide, homicide or without a medical doctor present, an autopsy may be required by law.

"Gift of Life"

3) To grant a request for vital organs to be used to help the living is a humanitarian idea. Many states provide channels (such as the Department of Motor Vehicles) for donating all or parts of one's body to science for transplants.

If you wish to leave organs or tissues to aid the living, or wish to leave your body to a medical school, you have the responsibility to let your next of kin know and make arrangements ahead of time.

Memorial

4) A memorial service is a service held after the body has been removed. Traditionally, family and friends gather to pay their respects and celebrate the life and memory of the deceased. Those who live on have an opportunity to express their grief and sorrow and hear words and songs of comfort.

A memorial service can be held at any time convenient to the family in a park, union hall, home, church, mortuary . . . after the body has been cremated or interred. The service usually includes music, responsive readings, a eulogy, selections from appropriate poetry or prose, comments about the person — her life, contributions, relevant work and values. Survivors have an opportunity to meditate on the meaning of life and death and share rituals that offer comfort and solace.

Funeral

5) By definition, a funeral is a service held in the presence of the body and can be held at a mortuary, church, home, union hall, lodge . . . A dignified, simple and economical funeral can meet the social and emotional needs of family and friends. Usually, the casket is closed and the family can hold a short service of committal afterward at the cemetery, or the body can be cremated after the funeral.

You may design any service you wish, but expensive and ostentatious funerals reflect the commercialization of death. Focus the service on the life of the one who has died and the healing process for the survivors. A photograph and/or other memento(es) of the deceased may be displayed and the service can include music, prose, poetry, readings, talks, responsive readings, meditation, eulogy . . .

Grave site Committal

6) Instead of a funeral or after a funeral, a short service may be held at the grave site. Usually this is for family and close friends only and arrangements for transportation to accompany the body (or the ashes) to the cemetery should be made in advance.

A grave site service provides a closure/a leave-taking which gives the family an opportunity to say farewell, start the filling of the grave, and hear words of comfort.

Cremation

7) Cremation is an economical, aesthetic, clean process for returning the body to the elements. Cremation is increasingly being used because ashes may be stored indefinitely, mailed for distant interment, kept in an urn or easily scattered.

A casket is not required for cremation (which is actually 'calcination' — intense heat that reduces the body to clean 'ashes'). With cremation, ashes may be scattered in many places, such as an ocean, river or stream, flower garden, desert, or cemetery grave site. Ashes may be kept in an urn, placed in a mausoleum or interred at a cemetery. Check state laws as special arrangement may have to be made.

Tributes
8) When a person dies, family and friends often want to pay tribute to their memory in some tangible way. Flowers are sent, or a preferred option is to suggest that a contribution be made to some worthwhile cause in their memory.

For yourself, it is wise to select *right now* the cause, agency, church, organization, school . . . you wish contributions sent in your memory. (See "My Wishes," pp. 148-150.)

Wills
9) If you have not drawn up a will, do so now.

You may write a will out in longhand (holographic) which does *not* require attestation of witnesses, or you may type out a will (or fill out a printed form) and have it witnessed and dated by two adults. To save your survivors from legal complications and to make clear decisions about property and other important matters (such as saving your assets from going to the state), it is wise to have legal assistance when writing your last will and testament.

When a loved one dies, locate their will as quickly as possible and have it filed with the county court. (In California, the County Superior Court within 30 days after death.)

Expenses
10) The major expense is the cost of a funeral director and the burial or cremation. This can vary from several hundred dollars to several thousand dollars. Remember, an excessive display of flowers

and an expensive casket are unnecessary; do not be talked into an extravagant funeral or memorial service.

Cremation is less expensive than burial; many people want their bodies returned to earth in a "natural" manner and prefer a wood or corrugated box to the more expensive copper, bronze and stainless steel caskets.

To save money, you may obtain a transportation permit from the Health Department and transport the body directly to the crematory (in a station wagon or other appropriate vehicle)* and request an inexpensive simple wood or corrugated container for cremation. A funeral society will transport the body to a medical hospital, crematorium or mortuary at a reasonable cost. You can leave the body at most hospitals until burial or cremation.

The most expensive method of handling death is to use the services of a mortuary to transport and embalm the body, provide a family/or viewing room and a chapel for the funeral, etc.

Cemeteries vary in cost and usually charge extra for weekends and holidays. They require payment for opening and closing the grave, a funeral vault to house the casket and, often, concrete grave liners or metal vaults.

Trans-portation of Body

11) To send a body for interment in a distant place, check with AMTRAK, which is less expensive than Air Express. To transfer the body yourself, you need a signed Death Certificate and a permit from the Health Department which may require embalming or dry ice.

Sympathy Calls

12) When someone you know dies and you pay a sympathy call to the bereaved family, avoid asking details about the death, medical costs and other

*Some states require that *only* a licensed funeral director or "direct disposer" may transport a dead body.

personal questions.

Do ask if you can —
   *send flowers.
   *make a donation in commemoration of the deceased.
   *help with the service, provide food, meet a relative at the airport, take someone to lunch or dinner, come over to chat or do some household chore . . .

The right words are less important than sharing emotions, reassurances and strong, loving arms. Be a good listener.

State laws vary so check with your Health Department.

DECISIONS AND ARRANGEMENTS: CHECKLIST

32 QUESTIONS

Decide *who* will be responsible to:

Name

The Body

_____ 1. Contact a doctor or coroner for the Death Certificate?*

_____ 2. Make several copies of the Death Certificate?

_____ 3. Decide whether or not to have an autopsy?**

_____ 4. Locate instructions left by the deceased? (This may answer many of the following questions.)

_____ 5. Decide on cremation, burial or medical school disposition of body?

_____ 6. Arrange transportation of body to mortuary, crematorium, cemetery, medical university hospital and/or, if need be, to another city/ state/country?

_____ 7. Decide whether to have a memorial service, funeral and/or grave site burial?

_____ 8. If a funeral, decide whether or not to embalm the body, have an open or closed casket, and if there will be viewing of the remains?

_____ 9. Select clothing deceased will be buried in?

*A doctor or coroner must declare the person dead and sign a Death Certificate, which can be obtained from the doctor, coroner, hospital, Health Department, convalescent home, funeral society or mortuary. The Death Certificate is filed with the Health Department.

**An autopsy is required in case of suicide, homicide or accidental death. Check state law.

The Service

_____ 10. Select a location for the service?

_____ 11. Contact a church, union hall, lodge, park, cemetery, mortuary; minister, counselor, or person(s) to arrange for a memorial service, funeral and/or grave site burial?

_____ 12. Select wood, corrugated or metal casket/or, an urn or a place to scatter ashes?

_____ 13. Create and determine the order of service: music,* poetry, prose, eulogy, responsive reading(s), speaker(s) . . .? Contact people who will participate? Have program printed? Hand out programs at service?

_____ 14. Select and contact pall bearers and/or ushers?

_____ 15. Order and/or arrange flowers? Be in charge of flowers received? Dispose of flowers after the service?

_____ 16. Provide a photograph of the deceased and/or memento(es), and a guest book (with pen) for the service?

Mourners and Sympathy Calls

_____ 17. Make a list of immediate family, close friends, employer(s) or business colleagues, organizations she belonged to, neighbors, etc.

_____ 18. Contact people by telephone, telegraph, letter, etc. and inform them of the death and the time of service?

*Music can vary from Beethoven's *Seventh Symphony*, Second Movement (first third) or *Third Symphony (Eroica)*, Second Movement; Grieg's *The Last Spring*; MacDowell's "To A Wild Rose" from *Woodland Sketches*; Debussy's *Au Clair de Lune*; *Shenandoah*; Carolyn McDade's *Go Well My Friend, Coming Home* and/ or *What I Do I Do For You* (Surtsey Publishing); *This World* (The Malvina Reynold's Songbook, Schroder Music Co.); *I Did It My Way; Londonderry Air;* to *So Long, It's Been Good To Know You.*

_____ 19. If flowers are to be omitted, decide on cause, organization, agency, or appropriate fund for memorial gift?

_____ 20. Provide hospitality for visiting relatives and friends?

_____ 21. Supervise food?

_____ 22. Provide background music?

_____ 23. Take turns answering the door and the telephone, and keep a record of sympathy calls?

_____ 24. Write an obituary and put death notice in newspaper(s)?*

Finances

_____ 25. Locate the will? Contact executrix/executor? Contact attorney?

_____ 26. Locate insurance policy(ies) and contact insurance company(ies)?

_____ 27. Contact Social Security,** Union, Sorority, Veterans Administration, Employee Benefits and other providers of survivor benefits?

_____ 28. Contact bank(s), credit card and other installment business accounts and creditors?

_____ 29. Pay for expenses of the service — funeral society, mortuary, transportation . . .?

_____ 30. Select and make arrangements for gravestone, or engraving on urn, or mausoleum inscription?

*Obituary: Include age, place of birth, occupation, education, memberships, outstanding work, and survivors; give time and place of any service(s). If contributions are to be made to a charity or organization in lieu of flowers, designate the agency. Newspapers prefer black-and-white glossy photographs. Deliver in person or by phone to newspaper(s).

**Request Social Security send copies of "Request Information — Medicare Payment For Services to a Patient Now Deceased" form H.C.F.A. 1660 (8-81). This form accompanies first bills for Medicare payments and requires the signatures of two witnesses. Also request form for $255 burial benefit.

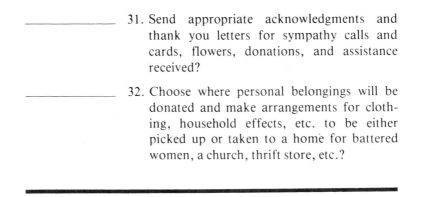

_____ 31. Send appropriate acknowledgments and thank you letters for sympathy calls and cards, flowers, donations, and assistance received?

_____ 32. Choose where personal belongings will be donated and make arrangements for clothing, household effects, etc. to be either picked up or taken to a home for battered women, a church, thrift store, etc.?

From WHEN LILACS LAST IN THE DOORYARD BLOOM'D

Come, lovely and soothing Death,
Undulate round the world, serenely arriving, arriving,
In the day, in the night, to all, to each,
Sooner or later, delicate death.

Prais'd be the fathomless universe,
For life and joy, and for objects and knowledge curious;
And for love, sweet love — but praise! praise! praise!
For the sure-enwinding arms of cool-enfolding Death.

Dark Mother, always gliding near, with soft feet,
Have none chanted for thee a chant of fullest welcome?
Then I chant it for thee — I glorify thee above all;
I bring thee a song that when thou must indeed come,
        come unfalteringly.

Over the tree-tops I float thee a song!
Over the rising and sinking waves — over the myriad
        fields, and the prairies wide;
Over the dense-pack'd cities all, and the teeming
        wharves and ways,
I float this carol with joy, with joy to thee, O Death!

                                    —Walt Whitman

WHEN THEY TOLD US THAT YOU HAD DIED. . .

When they told us that you had died quietly in your sleep we saw your face and the unbelievable became believable. We saw your face quietly, gladly, generously alive and the believable became bearable. The moment was one for our philosophies to turn to dust, as you forewarned, an ashed dust from which the Phoenix, life, rises, given time, but now waiting for confirmation of your name.

When they told us that you had died, we heard your voice as one hears music, beyond the meaning of the words to the intent. The burdened moment goes beyond explanations, lament, or eloquence, goes to the reaches of the music of your voice and the clarity of your face.

When they told us that you had died afar, we found your presence near, answering to our need, more friend than you could have guessed, more than we ourselves had known.

—Ernest H. Sommerfeld

> Live, I tell you,
> live, live, live.
> That's all there is!
> —Henry James
> *The Ambassador*

The life of the dead is placed in the memory of the living.

—Cicero
Philippicae No. ix, sec 5 (44 B.C.E.)

WHEN TO THE SESSIONS
OF SWEET SILENT THOUGHT

When to the sessions of sweet silent thought
I summon up remembrance of things past,
I sigh the lack of many a thing I sought,
And with old woes new wail my dear time's waste.
Then can I drown an eye, unused to flow,
For precious friends hid in death's dateless night,
And weep afresh love's long since cancelled woe,
And moan the expense of many a vanished sight.
Then can I grieve at grievances foregone,
And heavily from woe to woe tell o'er
The sad account of fore-bemoaned moan,
Which I now pay, as if not paid before;
    But if the while I think on thee, dear friend,
    All losses are restored and sorrows end.

—William Shakespeare

The end makes us all equal.

—Wm. Camden
Remains (1870)

WHY?

My tears come day and night
　I remember our times together.
For a part of me has died.
　As I remember, I pour out my soul.

Why? Why now?
　Why have I been forsaken?
Why must I mourn?
　Where is the healing?

mb

WILD GOOSE MESSAGE

Lament not yesteryear's spring
Gone ne'er to return again;
I have heard the wild goose o'erhead —
On descending air, this he said:
"Bury your heart at Wounded Knee, you say?
Take you a new heart, I pray you!
All honor to the noble brave and gone!
Be not less, or they may not rest!"
Into the cerulean distance they disappeared;
From cliff to cliff, faint echo rebounded,
"Say an orison for the wild goose!"

— Katie Burnett Nichols
a Miwok woman, elder of DQU
(1905 - 1976)
(Read at her funeral service in Sacramento, Ca.)

WHY DO WE HAVE TO DIE?

The still gray bird was lying on its side against the curb near our house.

IS IT DEAD, PAPA?

"Yes," I heard him say in a sad and distant way.

WHY DID IT DIE?

Everything that lives must die.

EVERYTHING?

Yes.

YOU TOO PAPA? AND MAMA?

Yes.

AND ME?

"Yes," he said. Then he added, "But may it be only after you live a long and good life."

The little boy could not grasp that everything alive would one day be as still as that bird. He forced himself to look at the bird.

WHY WILL EVERYTHING DIE, PAPA?

That's the way the world is made.

WHY?

— So life would be precious, my son. Something that is yours forever is never precious.

— Adapted from **My Name is Asher Lev**
by Chaim Potok
Alfred A. Knopf, Inc., 1972
Used at my grandfather's funeral:
Benjamin Byron Whiting (1877-1982), mb

WINTER

Life is so short
    so short —

      AND YET
      SPRING TO WINTER
      YOUTH TO AGED
      CAN SEEM
      A LONG, LONG TIME.

But when autumn ends —
   When the fragile light through the trees fade
   When the sweet smell of newly grown grass
      no longer comes to me —
   When I no longer feel the cool touch of water —
   When people call my name and I cannot hear —

      THE COLD LIGHT
      OF WINTER ASCENDS
      AND MY LIFE IS OVER,
      THE SEASONS SPENT.

Life is so fleeting
    so tenuous —

      SO PRECIOUS
      SO DEAR.

Cherish every moment
   Fill every day with sweet life
   For winter comes —

      SO SOON
      SO SOON.

Blessed Be.   mb

YOU

The world began the day you were born.
It will grow until you die.
If there are to be stars in your sky
You must put them there
If there are to be gods you must find them
If there is to be love
You must give it.

YOU ARE AT PEACE

She was born on _____ and she died on
_____. It is somehow comforting to state these facts. They
moor us to reality when all else seems unreal.

We will carry our memories in our heads and in our hearts.
We will believe that her life had meaning. We are left as custodians
of shared memories. We will re-live those memories clearly etched
on the rims of our eyelids.

Pass gently, dear _____. We know you are at
peace. We know you are a part of us. And we will carry our
memories wherever we go.

What's dying, but a kind of gilded sleep?
—S.V. Benet
Western Star, p. 42 (1943)

YOU CAN NOT TAKE IT WITH YOU

You can hoard all the gold that comes your way
    And store it in vaults, it is true;
But when the last gates are opened wide
    Not a bit can you carry through!

You can claim a deed to vast estates
    Where gardens and servants accrue—
But when Gabriel blows his trumpet blast
    Not a thing can you take with you!

You enter the world without a stitch
    And receive but a breath from the blue—
And when you go back from whence you came
    Even that is taken from you.

So with all the goods you accumulate
    On earth as you pass through—
None can be used wherever you go;
    Not a thing can you take with you!

                —Velta Myrle Allen

Life is greater than possessions.

GROWING OLD IS NO MORE THAN A BAD HABIT
WHICH A BUSY PERSON HAS NO TIME TO FORM.

YOU HAVE ONE DAY AT A TIME

One day at a time — this is enough,
    Do not look back and grieve over the past,
      For it is gone;
    And do not be troubled about the future,
      For it has not yet come.
    Live in the present,
      And make it so beautiful
    That it will be worth remembering.

                  —Ida Scott Taylor

We fall asleep and never wake again.
              —James Thomson
The City of Dreadful Night, Pt. xiv (1874)

YOU HAVE ONE LIFE

. . . We know so little about one another. A good bit of the time we spend hiding from one another — most of the time. And, too often we hide from ourselves, taking too little time for self care. We spend our lives learning how to protect ourselves from suffering, and yet the wisdom of our hearts calls us to the struggle to open ourselves, to risk, to be in the present moment, to know that part of living will include suffering but it is not too high a price.

Our self awareness is a blessing and a curse, but ultimately, and this is a part of my faith, it reveals that we are a self-transcending creature with more health in us than we sometimes know.

There is no doubt that we are at times fragile and in desperate need for a word of kindness, patience, understanding. But, there is a courage within, a health within. The Zen poet declared it in a way I love and upon which I am thrown back by this week's events, for I too believe

"Such is life,
Seven times down,
Eight times up!"

And, Anne Sexton in an equally bold fashion proclaims a courage in the human heart when she speaks in a poem titled "Courage" of

". . . you who have endured a great despair
. . . you powdered your sorrow,
you gave it a back rub
and then you covered it with a blanket
and after it had slept a while
it woke to the wings of the roses
and it was transformed."

It is so often a lonely thing, this business of living and dying, laughing and crying, loving and hurting. And sometimes it takes a good bit of energy to sustain ourselves, as much as we may try to have souls attuned to the moment to tap all the power which the grace of existence makes possible. Because it is so lonely, so much of the time, the more we can learn to "bear the beams of love," the more deeply we shall live.

Each of us has survived to this day. Since we have been given this reprieve, as my friend put it, what might we do today that we had only planned for the morrow? What word of kindness, of thanks, of appreciation, of tenderness must we continue to withhold? Why don't we begin to redeem the world today by our loving and our living?

—Rev. Bruce Southworth
The Community Church of New York
(Sermon Brief — March 17, 1985)

I never heard a dying person say — I should have spent more time on my business.

YOUR LIFE IS A JOURNEY

Birth is a beginning.
Death is a destination.
Life is a Journey

From childhood to maturity
  and Youth to Age
From Innocence to Awareness.

From Ignorance to Knowing
From Foolishness to Discretion
  And then perhaps to Wisdom.

From Health to Sickness and back,
  We pray, to Health again.

From Loneliness to Love
  From Pain to Compassion
    From Grief to Understanding
    From Fear to Faith —

Until looking backward or ahead
  We see that Victory lies
Not in some high place along the way
  But in having made the Journey.

Stage by stage —
  A sacred pilgrimage.

Birth is a beginning.
Death is a destination,
  And Life is a Journey.

Yes, Life is a Journey.
  A sacred pilgrimage.

                    —Unknown

A LIVING TRIBUTE:
FOR GAIL HAMAKER
(November 14, 1925 - February 15, 1986)

The time is right to initiate a ceremony to honor the living friend dying of a terminal illness. Unusual as it sounds, this can be an upbeat and joyous occasion. It is easy to do, especially if the ill person has an optimistic outlook. It can be even easier if the patient initiates the service herself (through a friend), thereby putting everyone positively at ease about a tribute to her while living rather than after she dies.

At a recent tribute for Gail Hamaker, she arrived dressed becomingly with her new wig coiffed attractively, and her seat of honor was made especially comfortable for her. The sponsor of the event asked each person to stand up and say a word or two about our honored friend: what each admired about her, how they met, what a difference knowing her has meant, etc. This was easily accomplished for we all were anxious to tell Gail of our admiration and love.

Song sheets had been printed for each to have and a leader roused us to some great singing of favorite songs. In our case, they were songs dealing with women's equality and spirituality and songs celebrating women, the topic of devotion to most of those present. An accompanist at the piano greatly facilitated the success of that segment of the evening.

When the invitations went out (by telephone in widening circles) about two weeks in advance, it was suggested that each friend, whether or not she could attend the event, send in a picture, a saying, a written tribute, a funny story, a recollection, or whatever expressed the sender's feeling. These items were collected prior to the event and inserted into plastic page holders and assembled into a great thick album and presented to the honoree that night for her to enjoy slowly and thoroughly in the coming days.

To close, we each held a lit candle in the darkened room and sang a Christmas carol (it was that season). Refreshments afterwards and individual greetings exchanged with our honored friend and others brought the evening to a memorable and touching conclusion.

—Alice Wallace

ESSAY

Death is one of two things: either it is a stage of nothingness and utter unconsciousness, or there is a migration of "the soul" from this world to another, one body to another, one generation to another, or wherever . . .

If there is no consciousness, but a type of deep sleep undisturbed by dreams, death is a gain; for eternity is then but a single night. It is reported that Walt Whitman hoped to become big and fat before his death so that his body would be rich fertilizer and perhaps a beautiful rose would grow above his grave. We *are* a link in the cycle of life.

But if death is also a journey, I hope it is *not* to a heavenly place where, as Mark Twain noted, thousands of tone-deaf people are making one huge cacophony trying to play a harp! If death is a journey to another state of consciousness, I hope it is to an interesting place where one meets one's grandparents and other loved ones who have gone before. What would be more fun? And, think of finding great musicians still composing; think of listening

"Personally, I don't believe in reincarnation. This myth about coming back as butterflies sounds ridiculous."

First appeared in *NEW WOMAN*.

to great discussions among the wise *a la* Steve Allen's television program, "Meeting of the Minds." Can you imagine joining Mary Wollstonecraft, Margaret Sanger and Elizabeth Cady Stanton as they reminisce about their life on earth? An eternity of growing wiser — more knowledgeable — would be heaven for me! And, I can understand why some people believe in reincarnation. What an exciting eternity to believe that you never really die, but get to return to this beautiful planet, in differing forms, over and over and over again!

Death is still a mystery, the unknown, and thus the basis of most religions today. We simply do not know the answers.

The hour of departure from this life — from this body — arrives and we go our separate ways —: I to die, and you to live. Which is better? No one knows. Bury my lifeless body where you please (or, spread by ashes where you please), but do not mourn. I am either asleep — with no pain, no nightmares, no consciousness — or I am atoms floating in the air —: or, (and I seriously doubt this) I dwell with the wise and good of all the ages, or will come back as a dog or a farmer or a teacher. These matters are nothing but conjecture.

So, celebrate my life! And as you come face to face with your own mortality, consider this world as a place Mother Earth never intended as a permanent abode, and if it makes you feel better, consider death an adventure as you journey to an unknown place. My last words to you are: As you face life day by day, treasure every moment for no matter what death *really* is, it comes too soon.

mb

> We grasp the slender thread of life.

MY WISHES

Full Name: _____ Date of Birth: _____

Birthplace: _____ Social Security No.: _____

Mother's Name and Birthplace: _____

_____

Father's Name and Birthplace: _____

_____

Names of Brothers and Sisters: _____

_____

_____

Name of Spouse (or Partner): _____

Date of Marriage(s) _____

Place of Marriage(s) _____

Marriage license(s) are located _____

_____

Marital Status: ☐ Single ☐ Married ☐ Widowed ☐ Divorced

My occupation and interests: _____

_____ Veteran: ☐ Yes ☐ No

My will may be found _____

Safety deposit box number is _____

Key is located _____

Bank: _____

Executrix/Executor _____

My closest relative is _____

Name and address of person(s) in charge of financial arrangements is ____

_____

I wish to have:

☐ My body cremated with a memorial service.

    I wish my ashes scattered over _____

☐ A memorial service with private burial before or after it.

☐ A funeral service with no graveside committal service.

☐ A traditional funeral with graveside committal service.

☐ A graveside committal service only.

I wish to be buried in _____ cemetery,

located at _____.

The deed to the burial lot is in the name of _____ and

the deed may be found_____.

I belong to the_____Funeral Society/Guild/Co-op

which is located at _____.

I wish to have my service held at:

☐ A church: I prefer _____.

☐ A funeral home: I prefer _____.

☐ In my own home.

☐ In a labor union hall; in a park; other directions: _____

_____

I would prefer that instead of sending flowers, my family and friends make

memorial gifts, if they wish, to: _____

I make the following suggestions of material which I would like to have used in my service:

Responsive readings:_____

Poems: _____

Songs:_____

Other music: _____

Speakers and other suggestions: _____

_____

☐ I would like to donate my eyes to the Eye Bank and have filled out a

card for this purpose and have sent it to: _____

_____

☐ I would like to give my body to:_____

_____

Other information: _____

_____

_____

Be sure to let someone know you have filled out *My Wishes* and where they can locate this booklet.

NOTES

NOTES

NOTES

NOTES

AN EXAMPLE OF AN OBITUARY:

This obituary from the *Idaho Statesman* reminds us that while death brings sadness, it can also bring peace and closeness to loved ones who still have their lives to live.

"Pamela Sue Goldsmith, 40 of Boise, died peacefully at 10 p.m. Sunday, shortly after sunset on Father's Day. During her six-month illness she received an enormous amount of love from her friends and family. Despite the illness, her last days were happy. We want to thank all who helped in so many ways.

"Memorial services will be held in the outdoors that Pam loved so much. She will be surrounded by green grass, tall trees and blue sky in Veteran's Park. The service will be conducted by family and friends. It will be a time to mourn, share memories, see old friends, heal ourselves and sing and celebrate the life of a wonderful woman. Please bring your memories of Pam's life to share with us.

"In spite of her fondness for fashion, Pam wore jeans and boots to her father's funeral because that is how her father always saw her and how she saw herself. Friends are invited to honor Pam by wearing their favorite clothes, casual or dress.

"Instead of sending flowers, we ask that you take a friend to lunch or dinner and tell him or her the things we often think of only after someone is gone."

THE SUNSHINE FROM OUR HOUSE IS GONE
WE FEEL TERRIBLY ALONE.

Each person is unprecedented, unrepeatable, and unique.
—Rene Dubos

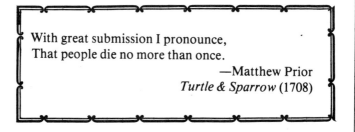

With great submission I pronounce,
That people die no more than once.
—Matthew Prior
Turtle & Sparrow (1708)

We are afraid to die, yet we are afraid to live.

With the dead there can be no more suffering.
—Sophocles
Trachiniae, 1.1173 (c.409 B.C.E.)